**"Double-pump, Slam dunk!"** Review.

"Everyone needs preparation. This certainly includes skilled young people getting involved with high level sports programs. The book *How to Play the Sports Recruiting Game and Get an Athletic Scholarship* is a big step toward preparation."
—Tom "Satch" Sanders, former Boston Celtic, eight time world champion NBA; Head Coach Boston Celtics '77-79; Head Coach Harvard University '72-76; currently Vice President, Player Programs, National Basketball Association

"Mom and Dad: This book is for you. It could save you a ton of money, just buy it!"
—Rob Parker, Sports Columnist, New York Newsday, New York

"As we approach the new millennium, with the high cost of collegiate aid, the *Sports Recruiting Game* is a must read for all prospective student-athletes."
—Coach Norwaine Reed, Former Coach Buena Vista High School '83-95, Saginaw, Michigan; sent over 100 players to the collegiate level

"Rodney McKissic captured the essence and delivered the tools that prepsters will need while pursuing their dreams. This easy-to-follow guide for parents and their children is the bible for the student athlete. A high school student-athlete without this book is like playing basketball below the rim. This how-to guide is a double-pump slam dunk. Get it. Read it. Study it. Follow it!"
—Branson Wright, Sports Writer, Grand Rapids Press; author of "Rookie Season"

"Rodney McKissic's book explains the recruiting process from A to Z. It should be required reading for all prospective student-athletes, their parents, coaches, and guidance counselors."
—Charles Payne, Former Assistant Mens Basketball Coach, University of California at Berkeley, MS Sports Management

"Whether an athlete is a blue-chip prospect, or Division II bound, the college recruiting waters can by choppy and confusing. *How to Play the Sports Recruiting Game* makes that ride smoother and puts the destination within sight. It is a MUST for parents of high school student-athletes."
—Rickey Hampton, columnist Flint Journal (Michigan)

"This is a great book for many reasons. The most important reason is that it teaches our kids how to play the game instead of the game playing them! This book is long overdue!"
—Byron Boudreaux, Assistant Basketball Coach, University of Washington

"*How to Play the Sports Recruiting Game and Get an Athletic Scholarship* is a tremendous asset to young African-American students and families to educate themselves about the process of achieving an academic, as well as an athletic scholarship to attend the university of their dreams."
—Steve Smith, Former Head Coach Men's Basketball, Dominican College of San Raphael. Currently Assistant Coach for WNBA Phoenix Mercury.

# Dedication

This book is dedicated to two future recruits,
Asher and Dru McKissic, and to all black athletes,
past, present and future who aspire to discipline,
dedication, academics, and greatness.

*Rodney J. McKissic*

"Like Mike, if I could be like Mike!"
—Popular 90s television commercial

# How to Play the Sports Recruiting Game and Get an Athletic Scholarship

The Handbook and Guide to Success for the African-American High School Student/Athlete

by Rodney J. McKissic

First Edition

Amber Books
Phoenix     Los Angeles, CA

# How to Play the Sports Recruiting Game and Get an Athletic Scholarship

The Handbook and Guide to Success for the
African-American High School Student/Athlete

by Rodney J. McKissic

Published by:
Amber Books
1334 E. Chandler Boulevard, Suite 5-D67
Phoenix, AZ 85048

E-mail: Amberbk@aol.com

## ALL RIGHTS RESERVED

Library of Congress Cataloging-in-Publication Data

McKissic, Rodney.
How to Play the Sports Recruiting Game and Get an Athletic Scholarship: The Handbook and Guide to Success for the African-American High School Student/Athlete / By Rodney McKissic—1st Ed.
p. cm.
Includes Bibliographical References and Index.
ISBN 0-9655064-1-X (Soft)

1. College Athletics—Recruiting—United States. 2. Afro-American Athletics—Scholarships, Fellowships, etc. 3. Universities and Colleges—United States—Admission—Planning. I. Title.

GV350.5.M33    1998
796'. 071' 173—DC21                                        97-4000
                                                              CIP

10 9 8 7 6 5 4 3

First Printing June, 1998

# Contents

# About the Author

Rodney McKissic is a sports journalist and a college basketball authority. He has written hundreds of articles for several newspapers, magazines and internet clients on sports and business. A graduate of the University of Cincinnati with a degree in broadcasting and a writing certificate in journalism, he is currently a sports reporter and copy editor for *The News Tribune* in Tacoma, WA. He is a beat reporter for the University of Washington men's basketball program and is *The News Tribune's* national college basketball writer.

# Personal Thoughts

I was inspired to write this book based on my time as a graduate assistant women's basketball coach at Grambling State University in 1992. During my experience, I felt a tool to assist student athletes in making the right decisions about which college to attend was desperately needed. I felt the student-athletes needed to be aware of all the options concerning their athletic, as well as their academic, careers and I view the bequest as an invaluable achievement. Yet landing the scholarship is only the beginning. The student-athlete is expected to work harder academically and strive for excellence. They are expected to lead and make sprightly decisions because everyone is watching. Above all, the student-athlete is expected to stay in good academic standing and graduate. The student-athlete should and can be a model for success.

# Acknowledgments

I wish to thank God and my Lord and savior Jesus Christ, through whom all things are made possible. Only the extraordinary support of my family and many, many others enabled me to see this project through. I am grateful above all, to my wife, Tracia, for her constant encouragement and generosity at every turn. I am indebted to the entire sports staff at *The News Tribune*, especially Arnold Lytle and Bill Schey for their editing expertise. To Robert Kuwada for his wealth of information and John Piekarski for the liberal use of his Macintosh SE. To Branson Wright, the man who helped make this endeavor possible, thanks for being my friend all these years. To my publisher and editor, Tony Rose, thank you for taking a raw venture and transforming it into something special. To all the athletes and coaches I met, my deepest thanks for your honesty, time and patience.

*Rodney J. McKissic*

The **Publisher** gratefully acknowledges those whose time, patience, help, and advice have contributed to the success of our literary efforts: Kay Bourne; Carol Herbert; Regina Thomas, whose belief in this book for high school student-athletes has been insurmountable; Wayne Summerlin, an extraordinary photographer; Cassandra Lattney; Yvonne David; Felicia Rose; Therese Fleetwood; Jamilla White; Florence Price; Erline Belton; the IBBMEC; the nation's African-American bookstores; our wholesalers and distributors; the black media; Yvonne Rose, whose faith and writing talents were our inspiration to begin this journey; and Rodney J. McKissic, whose love and respect for our high school student-athletes has given him the courage to write this book.

Book edited by Tony Rose
Cover and interior book design by Lisa Liddy, The Printed Page
Cover photo by Wayne Summerlin, Zoom Photography, New York
Cover athletes: Lance Singh–Manhattan High School of Math and Science, NYC, Football and Basketball; Althia Osbourne–Bishop Loughlin High School, Brooklyn, NY, Basketball; Darryl Lang–New York Automotive High School, Brooklyn, NY, Baseball and Basketball; Gaycia Jackman–Mount Pocono High School, Pennsylvania, Track and Field; Anis Hope–Transit Tech, NYC, Basketball; Shawna Singh, Bronx High School of Science, NY, Basketball and Volleyball

# Introduction

Each year, thousands of African-American high school athletes dream of being heavily recruited by college coaches and moving on to lyceum glory. It is an experience that can be flattering and enjoyable, with the prize being a scholarship at the school of your choice. Yet the road leading to a scholarship can be intimidating and perplexing.

In recruiting there is pressure which leads to questionable decisions by the student-athlete and everyone involved. Most of this stress, nevertheless, can be avoided if student-athletes and their families are schooled on the process carefully, clearly establishing their goals before one of the biggest games in their life begins. The more information you gather, the greater your chances of a recruiting victory.

This book is intended primarily for African-American student-athletes who want to participate in intercollegiate athletics. It is a how-to guide to help you, your parents, and coaches cope with the typical—and not so typical—dealings that occur during the recruiting procedure. Although this book peeks into the recruiting of men's and women's basketball and football, it can be read with interest by essentially any student-athlete who is seeking financial assistance from a university. This book features chapters that contain astute advice and observations from student-athletes, coaches, parents and media. These individuals were interviewed specifically for this book. It also contains the rules from the governing bodies of the National Collegiate Athletic

Association (NCAA), National Junior College Athletic Association (NJCAA) and the National Association of Intercollegiate Athletics (NAIA).

Numerous articles have been written about the evils and sins of recruiting, and some of the information gathered for this book paints a less than pretty picture on the topic. Nevertheless, many former student-athletes have taken their valuable athletic scholarships and blossomed into successful doctors, lawyers and teachers, among other affluent professions, as well as professional sports players. In many cases, these shining achievements could not have been possible without financial assistance through athletics.

There are many positive aspects regarding recruiting:  You can receive a free education, enhance your social life and, if talented enough, earn an opportunity to play professionally. These benefits also apply more and more to female student-athletes who are discovering professional athletic opportunities in the U.S. as well as overseas.

"Recruiting is put into a negative light, but without the recruiting and scouting that goes on, a lot of people wouldn't get opportunities," says the *Long Beach* (California) *Press Telegram's* Frank Burlison, one of the original members of the McDonald's All-American Game advisory committee for boys basketball. "How many people would know about the guys from the real small towns?"

With that in mind, recruiting can place an enormous amount of stress and pressure on the African-American student-athlete and his or her parents. The process can also cause an inflated sense of self-worth for nearly everyone involved.

"All these coaches are kissing the kid's butts for a couple of years and you lose perspective and what you're doing in the overall scheme of things," Burlison said. "Some guys' heads are totally screwed up. Everyone talks about how the kids get messed up, but I've seen some parents get real messed up too."

So how do you select the right school for you, one that is honest as well as athletically challenging and helpful? The biggest problem, most observers agree, is that too many people are doing the thinking for the student-athlete when it comes to college selection. With friends, relatives, coaches and college recruiters all pulling and tugging at the youngster, the pressure can be quite a burden. By studying this book, the student-athlete will be informed about the positives and negatives of college recruiting and be able to handle whatever problems that may occur.

If you know what you are seeking and have examined the school thoroughly, you will be in control of the situation. After reading this book, the student-athlete will be well informed on how to play the sports recruiting game.

*Photo by Lou Kit Wong*

In the 1950s, the African-American top athletes made thousands of dollars a year and usually had to take other jobs during the off-season. In the 90s, an African-American superstar athlete can earn millions. For example, the Los Angeles Lakers will pay center Shaquille O'Neal over $12 million during the 1997-98 season. In the 2002-03 season, O'Neal will receive over $23 million. What makes these African-American athletes so special and in demand? Well, besides their courage, skill level and poise, they all dedicated themselves to hard work, discipline, a determination to succeed.

The African-American athletes of today are responsible for hundreds of millions of dollars in profits for their franchises, agents and shoe companies, among others. In this introductory section, you will get to know some courageous and gifted athletes who paved the way, made the way, and some athletes you might know who are performing today.

# They Paved the Way:

**Kareem Abdul-Jabbar**, Basketball, UCLA – The former Lew Alcindor led UCLA to an 88-2 record and three NCAA titles (1967-69). In the NBA, Abdul-Jabbar was named to 19 All-Star teams and won six NBA titles with the Milwaukee Bucks and Los Angeles Lakers. With his lethal "sky hook," the 7-foot-2 Abdul-Jabbar scored an NBA record 38,387 points.

**Marcus Allen**, Football, USC – After starring as a quarterback and defensive back in high school, Allen won the Heisman Trophy as a running back in 1980. In his NFL career with the Los Angeles Raiders and Kansas City Chiefs, Allen has rushed for over 10,000 yards.

**Nate Archibald**, Basketball, Texas-El Paso – One of the best small players to ever play the game, "Tiny" starred at Texas-El Paso before beginning his brilliant pro career in Cincinnati in 1970-71. In 1972-73, Archibald led the league in scoring (34.0) and assists (11.4), the only player to ever accomplish that feat.

**Jim Brown,** Football, Syracuse – Simply the greatest football player of all time. Drafted first round, 1957, fullback to the Cleveland Browns. NFL's fifth all-time rushing leader (12,312 yards) and number one all-time leader in yards per rush (5.22). NFL champion, 1964. Voted in the Football Hall of Fame in 1971.

**Wilt Chamberlain,** Basketball, Kansas – Arguably the best center to ever play the game. A dominant player who spent two All-American seasons at Kansas before leaving for his senior year to play with the Harlem Globetrotters. During 14 NBA seasons, Chamberlain was the league MVP four times and still holds records in rebounds (23,924), season scoring average (50.4 in 1961-62) and most points in a game (100).

**Julius Erving,** Basketball, Massachusetts – One of the first to bring flash and style to basketball. He attended Massachusetts before beginning an extraordinary ABA career where he averaged 28.7 ppg., and 12.1 rpg., in five seasons. In 11 seasons with the Philadelphia 76ers, Erving averaged 22.0 ppg., and led the Sixers to the league title in 1983. Will be remembered for his leaping ability, dunks and cotton-candy style Afro.

**George Gervin,** Basketball, Eastern Michigan – One of greatest scorers to ever play the game. The "Iceman" was averaging 29.5 points per game before being expelled from school for hitting an opposing player during a brawl. The Virginia Squires of the ABA selected him in the first round in 1972 before the Squires sold him to the San Antonio Spurs. During his ABA/NBA career, Gervin scored over 26,000 points.

**Walter Payton,** Football, Jackson State – The greatest all-around running back in pro football history. "Sweetness" was drafted in 1974 by the Chicago Bears and led the NFC in rushing for five consecutive years from 1976-79. After leading the Bears to the Super Bowl title in 1986, Payton retired in 1987. He rushed for a league record 16,726 yards.

**Oscar Robertson**, Basketball, Cincinnati – One of the greatest all-around talent to ever play the game of basketball. Robertson was a three-time All-American at Cincinnati, where he remains the school scoring leader. As a pro, Robertson scored 26,710 points and recorded 9,887 assists.

**Bill Russell**, Basketball, San Francisco – Russell won two NCAA titles and 11 NBA championships with the Boston Celtics, and craved his reputation defensively. A true champion.

**Mike Singletary**, Football, Baylor – Scouts said he was too small to play linebacker in the NFL, but he used intensity, intelligence and desire to succeed in the NFL. Among the pantheon of Chicago Bears greats, Singletary was voted into the Pro Football Hall of Fame in 1998.

# They Made the Way:

**Florence Griffith-Joyner**, Track and field, UCLA – The fabulous "Flo-Jo" won the NCAA 200-meter championship in 1982 and the 400-meter title in 1983 for UCLA. She won three gold medals in the 1988 Olympics.

**Bo Jackson**, Football/Baseball, Auburn – Perhaps the greatest athlete in modern sports history. Jackson won the Heisman Trophy in 1985 and later became an All-Star outfielder for the Kansas City Royals and an All-Pro running back for the Los Angeles Raiders.

**Earvin "Magic" Johnson**, Basketball, Michigan State – At 6-9, Johnson was a point guard inside a power forward's built, yet dominated the game with his court sense. He led Michigan State to the NCAA tournament championship in 1979 and won his first of five NBA titles with the Los Angeles Lakers the following season. Magic is second in career assists behind Utah's John Stockton with over 10,000.

**Jackie Joyner-Kersee**, Track and field, UCLA – Attended UCLA on a basketball scholarship and was a four-year starter. She set college records in the long jump and pentathlon. Joyner-Kersee has won several Olympic gold medals in the long jump and heptathlon and is generally considered the best female athlete in sports history.

**Carl Lewis**, Track and field, Houston – Lewis won the NCAA long jump championship in 1980 and the 100-meter and long jump championships in 1981, but is best known for his Olympic glory. He won 10 Olympic gold medals before retiring from competition in 1996.

**Cheryl Miller**, Basketball, USC – The best female basketball player ever. Miller once scored 105 points in a high school game and was a four-time prep All-American. She was also a four-time time All-American at USC who led the Trojans to two NCAA tiles (1983-84).

**Warren Moon**, Football, Washington – He was left undrafted by the NFL and signed with the Edmonton Eskimos in 1978. He led Edmonton to six consecutive Grey Cup championships from 1978-83. In 1985 signed with the Houston Oilers and adapted easily to their run and shoot offense. In his NFL career Moon has passed for over 40,000 yards.

**Lawrence Taylor**, Football, North Carolina – An unparalleled combination of size, speed and power make Taylor the prototypical linebacker. Taylor played for two Super Bowl champions in 1986 and 1990 with the New York Giants and recorded 1261.2 sacks during his 13-year NFL career.

**Isiah Thomas**, Basketball, Indiana – A gutsy risk-taker who thrilled crowds with his flashy style and play making ability. Thomas led Indiana to the 1980 NCAA title and the Detroit Pistons to back-to-back titles in 1989 and 90. A warrior inside a 6-1, 180-pound body.

**Doug Williams**, Football, Grambling State – Became the first African-American quarterback to be drafted in the first round in 1977 by Tampa Bay. But Williams is perhaps better known for his dauntless display of courage in Super Bowl XXII when he threw four touchdown passes in the second quarter to lead the Washington Redskins past the Denver Broncos.

**Rod Woodson**, Football, Purdue – The prototypical defensive back, Woodson was an All-American at Purdue before being drafted by the Pittsburgh Steelers in 1987. He currently plays for the San Francisco 49ers as one of primary defensive weapons.

**James Worthy**, Basketball, North Carolina – At 6-9, 225-pounds, Worthy played like a man much smaller with his gliding moves to the basket. He won an NCAA title while at North Carolina, and three NBA titles as a member of the Los Angeles Lakers.

# Here Today:

**Charles Barkley**, Basketball, Auburn – Nicknamed the "Round Mound of Rebound" while attending Auburn because his weight often reached 300 pounds, Barkley slimmed down during his rookie season and has been an All-Star ever since.

**Barry Bonds**, Baseball, Arizona State – Bonds was an All-American outfielder at Arizona State and was chosen in the first round by the Pittsburgh Pirates. He played only 115 games in the minor before being called up during the 1986 season. Bonds is a three-time MVP and is now a member of the San Francisco Giants.

**Tim Brown**, Football, Notre Dame – Brown totaled 5,024 all-purpose yards at Notre Dame and won the coveted Heisman Trophy in 1987. He continued his all-around play as a receiver for the Los Angeles/ Oakland Raiders.

**Joe Carter**, Baseball, Wichita State – A two-time All-American at Wichita State, Carter entered the major leagues with the Chicago Cubs. He has spent the bulk of his career with the Toronto Blue Jays and hit a three-run home run in the ninth inning to win the final game of the 1993 World Series.

**Randall Cunningham**, Football, UNLV – The prototype of today's quarterback: tall, fast and athletic. Drafted out of UNLV in the second round in 1985, he became a starter the following season. A dangerous runner with a deft touch, Cunningham passed for over 3,400 yards in three consecutive seasons from 1988-90.

**Patrick Ewing**, Basketball, Georgetown – By the time he was a prep senior, Ewing weighed 240-pounds and stood 7 feet tall. He was heavily recruited and signed with Georgetown where he led the Hoyas to three Final Four appearances and one national title in 1984. Ewing has dominated the middle for the New York Knicks since 1985.

**Anfernee "Penny" Hardaway**, Basketball, Memphis State – Considered by many to be the next Magic Johnson, Hardaway has been an All-Star from the moment he was drafted by the Orlando Magic.

**Grant Hill**, Basketball, Duke – One of the best all-around players in the game today, Hill led Duke to the 1991 and 1992 NCAA championship and a runner-up appearance in 1994. He currently plays for the Detroit Pistons and is a perennial All-Star.

**Michael Jordan**, Basketball, North Carolina – The greatest to ever play basketball. As a freshman, Jordan hit the winning jump shot in the NCAA championship game in 1982 to beat Georgetown and has been winning ever since. Drafted by the Chicago Bulls in 1984, Jordan has scored over 21,000 points and won five NBA titles.

**Cortez Kennedy**, Football, Miami – Kennedy was an All-American defensive tackle in 1989 and was the third player selected by the Seattle Seahawks in the 1990 draft. Because of his amazing quickness for his size—6-3, 290-pounds—Kennedy is regarded as one of the game's elite defensive players.

**Steve McNair**, Football, Alcorn State – One of the most prolific passer to ever play college football. A three-time All-American at Alcorn State, McNair was drafted No. 3 overall by the Houston Oilers.

**Shaquille O'Neal**, Basketball, Louisiana State – Pure power and strength. A two-time All-American at LSU, O'Neal was drafted by the Orlando Magic in 1992. He led the Magic to the 1994 NBA Finals before signing a lucrative contract with the Los Angeles Lakers.

**Scottie Pippen**, Basketball, Central Arkansas – One of the game's best all-around talents, Pippen was drafted out of tiny Central Arkansas by the Seattle SuperSonics in 1987 and traded to the Chicago Bulls. Noted for his daring swoops and sallies to the basket, Pippen has helped the Bulls win five NBA titles during the 90s.

**Mike Powell**, Track and field, UCLA – Throughout his career, Powell was known as the second best long jumper behind Carl Lewis. But it is Powell, not Lewis, who holds the world record with a jump of 29 feet 4½ inches, beating the mark held by Bob Beamon by two inches.

**Jerry Rice**, Football, Mississippi Valley State – Generally regarded as the best wide receiver to ever play the game. Rice was a two-time All-American at tiny Mississippi Valley State and was selected in the first round by the San Francisco 49ers. Rice holds nearly every NFL receiving record.

**David Robinson**, Basketball, Navy – Robinson entered the Naval Academy in 1984 at 6-4 and left a 7-1 All-American center. He has been a dominating player from the moment he stepped on the court for the San Antonio Spurs.

**Barry Sanders**, Football, Oklahoma State – Sanders rushed for 2,628 yards his junior year and captured the Heisman Trophy before turning pro. He was drafted by the Detroit Lions and Sanders speed and elusiveness make him one of the game's great backs.

**Deion Sanders**, Football/Baseball, Florida State – Nicknamed "Prime Time" because of his ability to shine in the spotlight, Sanders is a two-sport star in the mold of Bo Jackson. Perhaps the great cornerback to ever play the game, Sanders is also a master at base stealing on the diamond. An athlete in the purest form.

**Bruce Smith**, Football, Virginia Tech – The first pick overall after a stellar career at Virginia Tech, Smith has the knack for making big plays, especially sacks. A perennial All-Pro defender, Smith plays for the AFC Champion, Buffalo Bills.

**Emmitt Smith**, Football, Florida – Not extremely fast, Smith uses quick moves and power to gain the majority of his yards. The anchor of a Dallas Cowboys franchise which dominated in the 90s.

**Dawn Staley**, Basketball, Virginia – A four-year starter at Virginia, Staley won the Naismith Trophy in 1991 and 1992. She was a key component on the 1996 Olympic Team and is a star in the American Basketball League.

**Frank Thomas**, Baseball, Auburn – A college All-American at Auburn in 1989, Thomas joined the Chicago White Sox during the 1990 season. Is best known for his mammoth home runs and his massive build. Thomas is the first player since Babe Ruth to have more than 100 RBI and more than 100 walks in each of his first three seasons.

**Sheryl Swoopes**, Basketball, Texas Tech – Handed in one of the most complete performances in NCAA history with a 44-point effort against Ohio State to win the 1993 NCAA championship for Texas Tech.

# The Top Black Sports Colleges and Coaches

These universities and colleges have provided our nation with some fine and exceptional student-athletes. The men and women graduates of these prestigious schools have enriched our lives through their dedication and discipline to academics and sports. A scholarship to any of these schools, and to any school of higher education, will provide you with a lifetime of invaluable experience and knowledge.

For information regarding applications, brochures, school history, former athletic alumni, and current school athletes, call the numbers listed below.

**Alabama A&M University—Alabama**
Men's Basketball: Vann Pettaway
Women's Basketball: Press Parham
Football: Kenneth Pettiford
(205) 851-5000

**Alabama State—Alabama**
Men's Basketball: Rob Spivery
Women's Basketball: Ron Mitchell
Football: Hampton Smith
(205) 293-4286

**Albany State College—Georgia**
Men's Basketball: Oliver Jones
Women's Basketball: Robert Skinner
Football: Hampton Smith
(912) 430-4600

**Alcorn State University—Mississippi**
Men's Basketball: Dave Whitney
Women's Basketball: Shirley Walker
Football: Cardell Jones
(601) 877-6100

**Arkansas Pine-Bluff—Arkansas**
Men's Basketball: Harold Blevins
Women's Basketball: Kenneth Conley
Football: Lee Hardman
(501) 543-8492

**Buthane-Cookman College—Florida**
Men's Basketball: Horace Broadnax
Women's Basketball: Rosina Pearson
Football: Alvin Wyatt, Sr.
(904) 255-1401

**Bowie State College—Maryland**
Men's Basketball: Taft Hickman
Women's Basketball: Edward Davis
Football: Sherman Wood
(301) 464-3000

**Clark Atlanta University—Georgia**
Men's Basketball: Anthony Witherspoon
Women's Basketball: Angelene Brown
Football: Willie E. Hunter
(404) 880-8000

**Coppin State College—Maryland**
Men's Basketball: Ron "Fang"
Mitchell
Women's Basketball: Brit King
(301) 333-5990

**Delaware State College—
Delaware**
Men's Basketball: James DuBose
Women's Basketball: Jackie DeVane
Football: John McKenzie
(302) 736-4901

**Elizabeth City State University—
North Carolina**
Men's Basketball: Barry Hamler
Women's Basketball: Vanessa Taylor
Football: Elisha Harris
(919) 273-4431

**Fayetteville State University—
North Carolina**
Men's Basketball: Ricky Duckett
Women's Basketball: Eric Tucker
Football: Jerome Harper
(919) 486-1141

**Florida A&M University—Florida**
Men's Basketball: Mickey Clayton
Women's Basketball: Claudette
Farmer
Football: Billy Joe
(904) 499-3000

**Fort Valley State College—
Georgia**
Men's Basketball: Michael Moore
Women's Basketball: Lonnie Bartley
(912) 825-6211

**Grambling State University—
Louisiana**
Men's Basketball: Lacey Reynolds
Women's Basketball: David Ponton
Football: Doug Williams
(314) 247-3811

**Hampton University—Virginia**
Men's Basketball: Steve Merfield
Women's Basketball: Patricia Bibbs
Football: Joe Taylor
(804) 727-5384

**Howard University—Washington,
DC**
Men's Basketball: Mike McLeese
Women's Basketball: Sanya Tyler
Football: Steve Wilson
(208) 806-2500

**Jackson State University—
Mississippi**
Men's Basketball: Andy Stoglin
Women's Basketball: Andrew
Pennington
Football: James Carson
(601) 968-2121

**Johnson C. Smith University—
North Carolina**
Men's Basketball: Steve Joyner
Women's Basketball: Hythia Evans
Liebert
Football: Daryl McNeil
(704) 638-5500

**Kentucky State—Kentucky**
Men's Basketball: Thomas Snowden
Women's Basketball: Antonio Davis
Football: George Small
(800) 325-1716

**Livingstone—North Carolina**
Men's Basketball: Charles
McCullough
Women's Basketball: Andrew
Mitchell
Football: Thomas R. Abrams
(704) 638-5552

**University of Maryland Eastern
Shore—Maryland**
Men's Basketball: Lonnie Williams
Women's Basketball: Joyce Jenkins
(301) 651-2200

**Mississippi Valley State
College—Mississippi**
Men's Basketball: Lafayete Stribling
Women's Basketball: Jessie Harris
Football: Larry Donsey
(601) 254-9041

**Morgan State College—Maryland**
Men's Basketball: Chris Fuller
Women's Basketball: Darcell Estep
Football: Stump Mitchell
(301) 444-3333

**Norfolk State—Virginia**
Men's Basketball: Michael Bernard
Women's Basketball: James Sweet
Football: Darnell Moore
(804) 683-8600

**North Carolina AT&T
University—North Carolina**
Men's Basketball: Roy Thomas
Women's Basketball: Selma Pinniz
Football: Bill Hayes
(919) 683-6100

**North Carolina Central—North
Carolina**
Men's Basketball: Gregory D.
Johnson
Women's Basketball: Joli Robinson
Football: Larry Little
(915) 560-6080

**Paine College—Georgia**
Men's Basketball: Ron Spry
Women's Basketball: Robert Skinner
(404) 821-8200

**Prairie View A&M—Texas**
Men's Basketball: Elwood Plummer
Women's Basketball: Robert Atkins
Football: Hensley Sapenter
(409) 857-3311

**St. Augustine's College—North
Carolina**
Men's Basketball: Norvell Lee
Women's Basketball: Dr. Bev
Downing
(919) 828-4451

**St. Pauls College—Virginia**
Men's Basketball: Edward Joyner
Women's Basketball: Rhoda Lewis
(703) 848-3111

**Shaw University—North Carolina**
Men's Basketball: Keith Walker
Women's Basketball: Bobby
Sanders
(919) 546-8200

**South Carolina State College—South Carolina**
Men's Basketball: Cyrus "Cy" Alexander
Women's Basketball: Keshia Campbell
Football: Willie Jeffries
(803) 536-7000

**Southern University—Louisiana**
Men's Basketball: Tommy Green
Women's Basketball: Herman Hartman
Football: Pete Richardson
(504) 771-2430

**Tennessee State—Tennessee**
Men's Basketball: Frankie Allen
Women's Basketball: Teresa Lawrence Phillips
Football: L.C. Cole
(615) 963-5105

**Texas Southern University—Texas**
Men's Basketball: Robert Moreland
Women's Basketball: Peggie Stapleton
Football: William Thomas
(713) 527-7011

**Tuskegee University—Alabama**
Men's Basketball: Ben Jobe
Women's Basketball: Jennifer Murphy
Football: Rick Comegy
(205) 727-8011

**Virginia State University—Virginia**
Men's Basketball: Ralph Traynham
Women's Basketball: Peggy Davis
(804) 257-5600

**Virginia Union University—Virginia**
Men's Basketball: Dave Robbins
Women's Basketball: Moses Galalt
Football: Williard Baily
(804) 257-5600

**Winston Salem State—North Carolina**
Men's Basketball: Sam Hanger
Women's Basketball: Debra Clark
Football: Kermit Blount
(919) 750-2000

# Women in Basketball

The surge of women's basketball didn't happen overnight.

The sport hit a lull for nearly a decade following the titillating Cheryl Miller-era with USC in the early to mid-80s. Then Sheryl Swoopes laid the foundation for another popularity boost with her dauntless 47-point effort in the NCAA tournament championship game for victorious Texas Tech in 1993. A year later, led by its Phi Beta Kappa star, Rebecca Lobo, Connecticut, made a giddy run to the national title with a 35-0 season.

The popularity of women's basketball is captured in Sheryl Swoopes, Lisa Leslie and the rest of the USA's barnstorming National Team that was preparing for the 1996 Olympics. The National Team— thought to the be the finest the U.S. has ever assembled—played in front of packed gyms and later won the gold medal.

Principals involved in women's basketball banked on the momentum from the 1996 Summer Olympics in Atlanta to create fan and corporate interest and therefore march the sports into a new era of professional leagues in the United States.

They were correct.

The American Basketball League (ABL) began in the fall of 1996 and the Women's National Basketball Association (WNBA) started in the summer of 1997.

The ABL was launched by a group of people who shared a common interest: Their teenage daughters loved playing basketball.

The average salary is $70,000, but the players own 10 percent of the league in a form called "The Player's Trust." and premier players like former Stanford All-American Kate Starbird and UConn star Kara

Wolters reportedly earn salaries in the millions. The league has teams located in Seattle, Portland, Long Beach, Denver San Jose, Atlanta, Columbus, Hartford, Conn./Springfield, Mass., and Philadelphia.

Before the ABL, top college seniors had to play overseas where salaries ranged from $50,000-$200,000. Nine members of the U.S. team played professionally in eight different countries in 1995.

While the ABL's strength is in its players, the WNBA's strength is in its marketing and advertising. The NBA, which acts as the marketing arm of USA Basketball, reportedly raised nearly $4 million through its deep bench of corporate sponsors. They signed players like Swoopes, Lobo and Leslie and dipped into the past for older stars like Nancy Lieberman-Cline and Lynette Woodard. And Miller, perhaps the greatest of them all, coaches the franchise in Phoenix.

With Tennessee State University's Tequila Holloway and Cari Hassell leading the way to a new generation of women basketball players and fans, professional women's basketball is here to stay.

## On Which Level Do I Belong?

If you're among the over six million student-athletes now participating on the high school level, you probably aspire to play at a Division I school in The National Collegiate Athletic Association (NCAA). In reality, only a few spots are open each year with thousands of qualified athletes eager to fill them. The NCAA is made up of 902 schools classified in three divisions.

Let's take a look at how the NCAA is classified:

## NCAA Division I

This is the highest level of competition for the student-athlete. Schools such as Duke, Kansas, UCLA and Florida fall into this category. In all, there are 305 schools in Division I.

By the 1997-98 school year, Division I schools must offer at least seven varsity sports for men's and women's teams. All Division I schools are in the same classification in every sport except football which is divided into two divisions (I-A and I-AA). For example, Louisiana State, a Division I-A school, may not believe you are big enough to play linebacker at its school, but Alcorn State, a I-AA school, says you have enough size to compete at its level.

Many top flight professional athletes have participated on the Division I level including Chicago Bulls star Michael Jordan (North Carolina), the Detroit Pistons forward Grant Hill (Duke) and Detroit Lions running back Barry Sanders (Oklahoma State). There are also stars from lower-level Division I schools who reached stardom professionally including Seattle SuperSonics All-Star Vin Baker (Hartford).

In Division I-AA, the degree of competition falls slightly, but some of the National Football League's greatest performers have participated on this level. Former Chicago Bears running back and Hall of Famer Walter Payton (Jackson State), Houston Oilers quarterback Steve "Air" McNair (Alcorn State) and San Francisco 49ers wide receiver Jerry Rice (Mississippi Valley State) have all played at Division I-AA schools.

## NCAA Division II

For student-athletes whose talents are not suited for Division I, another alternative is Division II. A notch below Division I, these schools must offer four varsity sports for men and women.

The number of scholarships available is lower than Division I, but coaches actively seek out qualified student-athletes. In all, there are 246 Division II schools.

Two players who played in the NFL from Division II schools include former Philadelphia Eagles' player Heath Sherman and Phoenix Cardinals star Johnny Bailey, who both played at Texas A&I. New York Knicks All-Star forward Charles Oakley (Virginia Union) was the nation's top rebounder in Division II during the 1984-85 season.

## NCAA Division III

A student-athlete's final option for playing in the NCAA is Division III, which doesn't offer full athletic scholarships. However, a student-athlete can apply for numerous financial-aid packages through the university.

Division III schools must offer four varsity sports for men and women. The route to the professional ranks is considered a long shot, but Division III gives you an opportunity to compete on the college level.

## NJCAA

Perhaps you possess the ability to play on the NCAA Division I level, but your academic standing isn't up to par according to the NCAA bylaws. Or, perhaps you are a late bloomer and your talents could use a little more seasoning. The National Junior College Athletic Association (NJCAA) is another option.

NJCAA members are two-year institutions commonly known as junior colleges, jucos or JC's. Attending a junior college will enable you to get your academic standing up to a level accepted by the NCAA, and in many cases assist in your maturation as a student-athlete. After completing two years at a juco, you should be able to handle the rigors of a four-year institution. Many NJCAA schools provide athletic scholarships, and its membership includes 540 institutions of higher learning.

The list of student-athletes who have participated on the juco level, then blossomed to become stars at NCAA Division I schools and the professional ranks, is long and impressive. In the NFL, 1983 Heisman Trophy winner Mike Rozier (Coffeyville (Kansas) Community College and Nebraska) was junior college student-athlete. In the NBA, Larry Johnson (Odessa (Texas) Junior College and UNLV) and the Los Angeles Lakers Nick Van Exel (Trinity (Texas) Valley Junior College and Cincinnati) were junior college stars.

## NAIA

Yet another option is participating at a school in the National Association of Intercollegiate Athletics (NAIA). The NAIA offers national championships in sports such as football, basketball, soccer, tennis, wrestling, and track and field. Some of these four-year institutions offer athletic scholarships and include approximately 425 fully accredited colleges and universities throughout the country.

The professional scouts also search the NAIA ranks for budding stars. The five-time World Champion Chicago Bulls have two former NAIA All-Americans on their roster in Scottie Pippen (Central Arkansas) and Dennis Rodman (S.E. Oklahoma State). Denver Nuggets center Priest Lauderdale was a first-round pick out of tiny Central State University in Ohio.

## Finding the proper level of competition

There are several steps you must take to make certain that you are recruitable. The first begins with a self-evaluation. Are you truly good enough to compete on the college level? Any athlete with confidence will instinctively answer "Yes." You've probably already visualized yourself running for touchdowns on Saturday afternoon, or draining 3-pointers at the buzzer to win the conference championship. Yet sometimes, we truly have to take a hard look at ourselves and see if this dream can become a reality.

The first step is to talk with your coach and guidance counselor to see where you stand academically and athletically. Your counselor should be able to obtain information regarding college-entrance requirements and other pertinent information on schools. The counselor should also be able to inform you if your grades are high enough to attend a certain university. For example, NCAA Division I school Stanford University has strict academic requirements for incoming freshmen, but Arizona State University's guidelines may be more relaxed, therefore allowing you the opportunity to gain admission. But keep in mind you become much more attractive to recruiters if you have a 3.5 GPA with a 1000 SAT score. It is extremely important to realize that the NCAA has tough requirements for incoming freshmen student-athletes.

## Recruiting Requirements

You become a prospective student-athlete if you have started classes for the ninth grade. Before the ninth grade, you become a prospective student-athlete if the college provides you (or relatives or friends) any financial aid or other benefits that the college does not provide to the general student body. For example, if you are given a T-shirt from a particular school, you are considered a prospective student-athlete.

You are considered a recruited prospective student-athlete at a college if any college coach or representative of the college's athletic program shows interest and solicits you for the purpose of securing your enrollment and participation in athletics at that college. Activities by coaches or athletics representatives that cause you to become a recruited prospective student-athlete include, but are not limited to, the following:

❑ 1. Providing the student-athlete with transportation to the college campus.

❑ 2. Entertaining you or any member of your family in any way (meals, tickets, movies, lodging, rides, etc.) on or off campus. You may receive a complimentary admission to an athletic event on campus when you visit with a group, such as your high-school team.

❑ 3. Placing telephone calls to your family anywhere other than the college campus.

❑ 4. No alumni or representatives of a college's athletics interests can be involved in your recruiting. There can be no telephone calls or letters from boosters. The booster restriction does not apply to recruiting by alumni or representatives as part of a college's regular admissions program for all students.

❑ 5. You and your family may not receive any benefits, inducements, or arrangements such as cash, clothing, cars, improper expenses, transportation, gifts or loans to encourage you to sign a National Letter of Intent or to attend a school.

❑ 6. A college coach may contact you in person off the college campus only on or after July 1 after completion of your junior year of high school. In football, telephone calls from faculty members and coaches are not permitted until on or after August 15 after completion of your junior year.

After this, a college coach or faculty member is limited to one telephone call per week to you (or your parents or legal guardians), except that unlimited calls to you may be made under the following circumstances:

❑ 1. During the five days immediately before your official visit by the college you will be visiting.

❑ 2. On the day of a coach's off-campus contact with you by that coach.

❑ 3. During the time beginning with the initial National Letter of Intent signing date in your sport through the two days after the signing date.

❑ 4. In football between December 1 and February 15 of your senior year, a college coach may telephone you as often as he wishes.

Coaches also may accept collect calls from you on or after July 1 after completion of your junior year. Enrolled student-athletes may not make recruiting telephone calls to you while you are a high school student-athlete at any time. Letters from coaches, faculty members and students are not permitted until September 1 at the beginning of your junior year in high school.

Any face-to-face meeting between a college coach and you and your parents or guardian, during which any of the party says more than "hello" is considered a contact. Also, any face-to-face meeting that is prearranged, or that occurs at your high school or at any competition or practice site is a contact, regardless of the conversation. These contacts are not permissible "bumps." If you meet a coach and say more than "hello," that is a contact.

In all sports, coaches may contact you off the college campus a total of three times at any site. However, a coach may visit your high school, with the approval of the your high-school principal, only once during a particular week during a contact period. In football, coaches from a college may visit at your high school on no more than three days during the football contact period.

## Walk-ons

Student-athletes who attempt to participate on the college level without the benefit of an athletic scholarship are generally referred to as walk-ons. They are called walk-ons because they tryout for the team, most of the time without a firm invitation, in hopes of making the team. Many schools need walk-ons to fill out their roster, especially non-revenue sports such as field hockey and tennis. Most of these athletes receive little, if any playing time, but there are exceptions. The Virginia Tech football team, for example, uses walk-ons to assemble their offensive line. In the Notre Dame basketball media guide, a special section is devoted specifically for records by walk-ons.

Perhaps the most successful walk-on story ever is by Utah Jazz guard Jeff Hornacek. Hornacek walked-on to the Iowa State basketball program in 1983 and four years later he was drafted in the second-round by the Phoenix Suns. He is one of the game's best medium-range jump shooters, and an important reason why Utah advanced to the NBA Finals in 1997.

## Evaluations

An evaluation is any off-campus activity designed to assess your academic standing or athletic ability. This includes any visit to your high school, during which no contact occurs, or the observation of any practice or competition in which you participate. In all sports, coaching staff members may evaluate you on no more than four occasions each year. These dates include:

❑ 1. For Division I-A and I-AA football, from May 1 through April 30 of the following school year.

❑ 2. Throughout the school year in all sports other than football. All competition that occurs on consecutive days within a tournament, and normally at the same site, or that involve a tournament setting counts as a single evaluation.

In football and basketball there are specified periods when a coach may contact you off the college campus and/or attend your practices and games in order to evaluate your talent level. The NCAA Council may waive the contact periods for schools with established admission dates that occur after the normal contact deadline.

A Division I school attempting to recruit you may provide the following printed materials but only on or after September 1 at the beginning of your junior year in high school:

❑ 1. Official academic, admissions, and student services publications published by the school.

❑ 2. One annual athletics publication.

❑ 3. One student handbook.

❑ 4. One wallet-size playing schedule per sport.

❑ 5. Drug-testing information.

❑ 6. Summer-camp brochures.

❏ 7. General correspondence, including letters and regular cards that do not include pictures of the school's department of athletics personnel or enrolled student-athletes.

❏ 8. Newspaper clippings, which may not be assembled in any form of a scrapbook.

❏ 9. Any necessary pre-enrollment information regarding orientation, conditioning, academics and practice activities, provided a student-athlete has signed a National Letter of Intent or has been accepted officially for enrollment by a school that does not subscribe to the National Letter of Intent program.

# Contact Periods for:

| | |
|---|---|
| **Football** | December and January |
| **Men's Basketball** | September, March and April |
| **Women's Basketball** | September, March and April |

# Evaluation Periods for:

| | |
|---|---|
| **Football** | October, November and May |
| **Men's Basketball** | July and November |
| **Women's Basketball** | July, October and February |

[**Note:** There's a "dead" period (when coaches may not contact or evaluate you on or off the college campus) in all sports 48 hours before and 48 hours after 7 a.m., on the initial National Letter of Intent signing date.]

For more information on the NCAA, NJCAA, NAIA, and the contact or evaluation periods write or call immediately:

NCAA
6201 College Boulevard
Overland Park, Kansas 66211-2422
(913) 339-1906

NJCAA
P.O. Box 7305
Colorado Springs, Colorado 80933-7305
(719) 590-9788

NAIA
1221 Baltimore Avenue
Kansas City, Missouri 64105
(816) 842-5050

# The National Letter of Intent

The National Letter of Intent is administered by the College Commissioners Association, not the NCAA. There are some restrictions related to signing a National Letter of Intent that may affect your eligibility as defined by the NCAA.

1. An NCAA member may not participate in an institutional or conference financial-aid agreement that involves a signing date that precedes the initial signing date for the National Letter of Intent program in the same sport.

2. **Mailing of Financial Aid Offer**. An institutional or conference financial aid form may be included in the normal mailing of the National Letter of Intent, but none of the forms enclosed in the mailing may be signed by you prior to the initial signing date in that sport in the National Letter of Intent program.

3. **Offer of Aid Prior to Signing Date**. An NCAA member may indicate in writing to you that an athletically related grant-in-aid will be offered by the institution. Nevertheless, the institution may not permit you to sign a form indicating your acceptance of such an award prior to the initial signing date in that sport in the National Letter of Intent program.

4. **Division III Letter of Intent prohibition**. A Division III institution, or one that competes in a sport in Division III, shall not utilize any form of a letter of intent similar to the form of commitment in the recruitment of you in a sport classified in Division III. Nevertheless, it

shall be permissible of the institution to utilize in your recruitment its pre-enrollment forms executed by prospective students in general at that institution.

Once you sign the Letter, you are bound to that school for one school year. If you decide that you don't want to attend that school, you must sit out one school year. If the school doesn't release you from your commitment, which is rare but it has happened, you must sit out two full school years.

In 1989, Lawrence Funderburke signed a basketball scholarship with Indiana University. The enigmatic Funderburke stormed out of one of coach Bobby Knight's practices and Hoosier basketball forever. After leaving IU, Funderburke announced he wanted to attend Louisville but Knight refused to release him from his Letter of Intent. He resurfaced at St. Catharine College (Kentucky), but didn't play basketball. Along the way, he was rumored to be headed to Kentucky or Tennessee. He later re-enrolled at Indiana for one semester before finally landing at Ohio State University and finishing up following the 1993-94 season. Funderburke's long and trying journey is a prime example of how important it is to select a school carefully.

There have been some cases where Letters of Intent have been broken and students did not have to sit out the school year. Former University of Tennessee basketball All-American Allan Houston originally signed a Letter with the University of Louisville as a high school senior where his father, Wade, was an assistant. Wade received a job offer as coach at Tennessee before Allan's freshman season, and the NCAA allowed Allan to join his father and not sit out a year.

In the fall of 1996, prep All-American Schea Cotton signed to play basketball at Long Beach State where he hoped to join his brother James. After James announced he was entered the NBA draft, Schea decided he no longer wanted to attend Long Beach State, and the school released him from his commitment. In the spring of 1997, Schea signed with UCLA.

You should read the National Letter of Intent document carefully. Any questions regarding the National Letter of Intent signing dates or restrictions related to signing the Letter should be addressed to the conference office of the college you are interested in attending. You can also gain more information by writing the CAA, c/o Southeastern Conference, 2201 Civic Center Blvd., Birmingham, AL, 35203.

## Signing Months

| Sport | Initial Month |
|---|---|
| Basketball: | |
|     Early Period | November |
|     Late Period | April |
| Football | February |
| All Other Sports: | |
|     Early Period | November |
|     Late Period | April |

Notes:

## Academic Eligibility Requirements

### NCAA Division I Academic Eligibility Requirements

If you're entering a Division I school on or after August 1, 1996, or thereafter, in order to be considered a qualifier for a scholarships, you're required to:

- ❑ 1. Graduate from high school.

- ❑ 2. Successfully complete a core curriculum of at least 13 academic courses. This core curriculum includes at least four years of English, two in mathematics, one year of algebra and one year of geometry (or one year of a higher-level math course for which geometry is a prerequisite), two in social science, two in natural or physical science (including at least one laboratory class, if offered by your high school) and two additional courses in English, mathematics or natural or physical science: and two additional academic course (which may be taken from the already-mentioned group, e.g., foreign language, computer science, philosophy.)

- ❑ 3. Achieve a grade-point average (based on a maximum of 4.000) and attain a combined score on the Scholastic Aptitude Test (SAT) verbal and mathematical sections or a composite score on the American College Test (ACT) based on index scale.

## Qualifier Index

| Core GPA | ACT | SAT |
|----------|-----|-----|
| Above 2.5 | 68 | 820 |
| 2.475 | 69 | 830 |
| 2.450 | 70 | 840-850 |
| 2.425 | 70 | 860 |
| 2.400 | 71 | 860 |
| 2.375 | 72 | 870 |
| 2.350 | 73 | 880 |
| 2.325 | 74 | 890 |
| 2.300 | 75 | 900 |
| 2.275 | 76 | 910 |
| 2.250 | 77 | 920 |
| 2.225 | 78 | 930 |
| 2.200 | 79 | 940 |
| 2.175 | 80 | 950 |
| 2.150 | 80 | 960 |
| 2.125 | 81 | 960 |
| 2.100 | 82 | 970 |
| 2.075 | 83 | 980 |
| 2.050 | 84 | 990 |
| 2.025 | 85 | 1000 |
| 2.000 | 86 | 1010 |

A partial qualifier is eligible to practice with a team at its home facility and receive a scholarship during his first year at a Division I school and then has three seasons of eligibility remaining.

A partial qualifier may earn a fourth of eligibility, provided that at the beginning of the fifth academic years following the student-athlete's initial, full-time collegiate enrollment, the student-athlete has received a baccalaureate degree. In order to be considered a partial qualifier you have not met the requirements for a qualifier, but you're required to:

❏  1. Graduate from high school

❑ 2. Present a grade-point average (based on a maximum of 4.0) and combined score on the SAT verbal and math section or a sum score on the ACT based on the following partial qualifier index scale:

| Core GPA | ACT | SAT |
|---|---|---|
| Above 2.750 | 59 | 720 |
| 2.725 | 59 | 730 |
| 2.700 | 60 | 730 |
| 2.675 | 61 | 740-750 |
| 2.650 | 62 | 760 |
| 2.625 | 63 | 770 |
| 2.600 | 64 | 780 |
| 2.575 | 65 | 790 |
| 2.550 | 66 | 800 |
| 2.525 | 67 | 810 |

# NCAA Division II Academic Eligibility Requirements

If you're entering a Division II college on or after August 1, 1996, or thereafter, in order to be considered a qualifier, you're required to:

❑ 1. Graduate from high school.

❑ 2. Have a GPA of 2.0 (based on a maximum 4.0) in a successfully completed core curriculum of at least 13 academic courses. This core curriculum includes three years in English, two in math, two in social science, two in natural or physical science—including at least one laboratory class, if offered by your high school—and two additional courses in English, math or natural or physical science; and two additional academic courses—which may be taken from the already-mentioned categories, e.g. foreign language, computer science, philosophy.

❑ 3. Have a combined score on the SAT verbal and math sections of 700 if taken before April 1, 1995 or 820 if taken on or after April 1, 1995, or a 68 sum score on the ACT.

A partial qualifier is eligible to practice with a team at its home facility and receive a scholarship during his first year at a Division II school.

In order to be considered a partial qualifier, you have not met the requirements for a qualifier, but you're required to graduate from high school and meet one of the following requirements:

■ Specified minimum SAT or ACT scores

■ Successful completion of a required core curriculum consisting of a minimum number of courses and a specified minimum grade-point average in the core curriculum.

# NJCAA Academic Eligibility Requirements

❑ 1. You must either be a high-school graduate, have received a high school equivalency diploma, or have been certified as having passed a national test such as the General Education Development Test (GED).

❑ 2. Non high-school graduates can establish eligibility for athletic participation by completing one term of college work passing twelve credits with a 1.75 GPA or higher. This term must be taken after the student-athletes' high school class has graduated.

❑ 3. Non high-school graduates who have earned sufficient credit for high school graduation status can establish athletic eligibility by completing one term of college work, passing twelve credits with a 1.75 GPA or higher. This term can be completed before the student's high school class has graduated.

❑ 4. Students classified under 2 or 3 above, may be added to the eligibility roster at any time after completion of the requirements in the respective sections.

❑ 5. Students who are completing high school and are simultaneously enrolled in twelve or more credits at a college are eligible for athletic participation with the completion of the NJCAA High School Waiver Form. This form must be signed by the high school principal, and the college president. This provision is applicable only to those students whose high school class has not graduated at the time of college enrollment.

# NAIA Academic Eligibility Requirements

Beginning in the fall term of 1989 you must, if you are a first-time entering freshmen, meet two of three entry level requirements:

- ❏ 1. A minimum score of 18 on the ACT or 740 on the SAT (740 SAT score effective August 1, 1993. Prior to August 1 enrollment, a 700 or better SAT was acceptable). Test must be taken on a national testing date. Scores must be achieved on a single test (residual tests are not acceptable).

- ❏ 2. Achieve an overall high school GPA of 2.000 on a 4.000 scale.

- ❏ 3. Graduate in the top half of your high school graduating class.

    a. The ACT/SAT test must be taken on a national testing date and certified to the institution prior to the beginning of the term in which you initially participate.

    b. A first-time entering freshman is defined as a student who upon enrollment is becoming identified with another institution of higher learning for two semesters or three quarters (or equivalent).

## Definition of a Core Course

A core course is defined as a recognized academic course (as opposed to a vocational or personal-services course) that offers fundamental instructional components in a specified area of study. Courses that are taught at a level below the high school's regular academic instructional level (remedial, special education or compensatory) can not be considered core courses regardless of course content. Seventy-five percent of the instructional content of a course must be in one or more of the required areas. The required areas include:

| | |
|---|---|
| *English* | Core courses in English shall include instructional elements in the following areas: grammar, vocabulary, development, composition, literature, analytical reading or verbal communication. |
| *Mathematics* | Core courses in mathematics shall include instructional elements in algebra, geometry, trigonometry, statistics or calculus. |
| *Social Science* | Core courses in social science shall contain instructional elements in history, social science, economics, psychology, geography, sociology, government, political science or anthropology. |

*Natural or Physical Science*
(including at least one full unit of laboratory classes if offered by the high school). Core courses in natural or physical science shall include instructional elements in biology, chemistry, physics, environmental science, physical science or earth science.

*Additional Academic Courses*
Units must be from courses in the above areas or foreign language, computer science, philosophy or non doctrinal religion (e.g., comparative religion) courses.

## Core-Curriculum Interpretations

❏  1. At Division I schools, generally only courses completed in grades 9-12 may be considered core courses. Courses taken after the completion of your eighth semester (summer school after the senior year) may not be used to satisfy core-curriculum requirements.

At Division II schools, you are permitted to use all core courses, completed before initial enrollment at a collegiate institution as certified on the official transcript or by official correspondence.

❑ 2. At Division I schools, a student-athlete who repeats an entire regular term or academic year of high school may utilize appropriate courses taken during that term or year to fulfill the core-course requirements. If the repeated term or year occurs after graduation, the core-curriculum courses utilized must be taken at the high school from which the student has graduated, and the student-athlete's initial full-time collegiate enrollment may not occur until the following academic year.

❑ 3. Eighth-grade courses may be used to satisfy core-curriculum requirements only if the courses taken in that grade are considered by the high school to be equivalent to courses normally taken in the ninth grade or above.

❑ 4. The core-curriculum grade-point average may be calculated using your 11 best grades from courses that meet the distribution requirements of the core curriculum grade-point average provided the distribution requirements are met. Student-athletes first entering college on or after August 1, 1996, must successfully complete 13 courses

❑ 5. You must present 11 different courses in meeting the core-curriculum requirements. A repeated course may be utilized only once. You may use the best grade in the repeated course in the calculation of the core-curriculum grade-point average. Student-athletes entering college on or after August 1, 1996, must successfully complete 13 courses.

❑ 6. Independent study or correspondence courses may not be used to satisfy the core-curriculum requirements.

❑ 7. Courses that are awarded pass-fail grades may not be used to satisfy the core-curriculum requirements.

❑ 8. Student-athletes entering a Division I or II school as freshmen must have satisfactorily completed all courses used to satisfy the core-curriculum requirements. Student-athletes must have a "D" or above.

❑ 9. A college course may be used to satisfy core-curriculum requirements if accepted by the high school, provided the course:

■ Would be accepted for any other student.
■ Is placed on the student-athlete's high school transcript.
■ Meets all other requirements for a core course.

❑ 10. A one-year course that is spread over two years is considered one course.

❑ 11. A course that is taken in preparation for the first course normally taken to fulfill the progression of core-curriculum requirements may not be utilized as a core course regardless of the content.

❑ 12. The principal of the high school from which the student graduated is the person who makes the decision as to whether a course qualifies as a core course. An NCAA school is responsible for verifying that the information received from the high school is valid.

❑ 13. High school courses for the learning disabled or handicapped may be used to meet the core-course requirement if the high school principal submits a written statement to the NCAA indicating that students in the courses are expected to acquire the same knowledge, measure and capacity as students in other core courses and that the same grading standards are employed in such courses as those utilized in other core courses.

Documentation that these conditions have been met must be produced to the NCAA Academic Requirements Committee, which then may recommend approval of the use of such courses on a case-by-case basis.

❑ 14. If you have completed a portion of your secondary studies in a foreign country, your academic record should be submitted to the NCAA's national office for review by the foreign-student records consultants.

## Test-score Requirements

In Divisions I and II, you must achieve the minimum required SAT or ACT score before your first college enrollment. Your test scores must be achieved under national test conditions on a national testing date.

Notes:

## Selecting Your School

Selecting a college is more than choosing a place to earn a degree and play basketball or football. For many student-athletes, it also means determining where you will work and live for most of the next four to five years of your life.

To help the student-athlete make that pivotal verdict, this chapter contains a list of questions to consider when you are choosing a college.

The Select-Your-College-Chart will assist you in evaluating each college you are interested in. In selecting a college, you should consider the following:

(I) Academic environment
(II) Social environment
(III) Campus environment
(IV) Athletic facilities
(V) Athletic program
(VI) Intangibles

Grade each criteria listed below from 1-10 with 10 being the highest possible score.

You should use this Select-Your-College-Chart on each of your final selections and grade them accordingly.

# Select-Your-College-Chart

## I. Academic environment

❑ **1. Reputation of the university.** Be certain that the college is highly regarded in your field of study.

❑ **2. What is the African-American enrollment?**

❑ **3. Intended major.** Does the college offer your major? If not, what's the closest subject?

❑ **4. If I do not declare a major, is the general studies program a quality one?**

❑ **5. Student-teacher ratio.** How many students will be in the classroom with you? Smaller classroom settings usually indicates a better student-teacher rapport.

❑ **6. Change of major.** Will you be allowed to change your major easily? Some student-athletes enter college with one major in mind then decide to switch to another.

❑ **7. Tutoring programs.** Does the athletic department pay for the service?

❑ **8. Counselors.** How many African-American counselors will be available to you?

❑ **9. Study Hall.** A university with a strong study-hall program is recommended. It gives you the opportunity to study in a quiet setting each day before or after practice, and can lead to stronger study habits.

❑ **10. Summer internships and co-op programs.** All student-athletes are not blessed with the ability to play on the professional level. Summer internship programs will assist you in planning for your future by giving you the opportunity to work in your field of study.

❏ **11. Regulations on student-athletes who fail to meet the NCAA's academic standards.** Some schools allow only a certain amount of Prop. 48 student-athletes each year. Others allow none.

❏ **12. Graduation rates.** By comparing the overall graduation rates of each university, you will discover which schools are indeed serious about academics, and which schools are lacking in their commitment to education.

## II. Social Environment

❏ **13. Attitude of the regular students.** Did it seem as if you were treated like any other student, or with an attitude as if you were a dumb jock? These are the students who will be seated next to you in class and you need to be in a comfortable setting.

❏ **14. Fraternities/Sororities.** Are there any traditional African-American fraternities or sororities on the campus?

❏ **15. Entertainment off campus.** Will you be able to hop in your car with your friends and travel to the local mall, museum, greasy hamburger hut, or night club?

❏ **16. Programs.** Does the school have any African-American programs geared toward your needs?

❏ **17. Is there a Black Student Union?**

## III. Campus Environment

❏ **18. Distance from home.** How far do you want to travel away from home? Will your family and friends be able to come see you play? Do you want to see another part of the country?

❏ **19. The library.** Does it have all the materials you need for the countless number of term papers you have to write? Is it a quiet place to think and study? How late does it stay open? It is extremely important that you attend a school with a high-quality library.

❏ **20. Campus transportation.** Some campuses have stepped into the 21st century and included bus systems because they are so large. Will you be able to walk to your classes on time?

❏ **21. Laundry facilities.** A word to the wise: Save yourself some embarrassment and learn how to do laundry *before* you go to college.

❏ **22. Living quarters.** You're 6-foot-10 and 350-pounds, will you be able to live comfortably in the dorm rooms? How big are they? How small are they? Will you be allowed to get an apartment off campus? You will be spending a lot of time in these rooms or apartments and it is essential that you live in a relaxed setting.

❏ **23. The resident advisor.** The RA is there to keep law and order in the dorm, but he can also become your friend and counselor.

❏ **24. Overall setting.** Are there a lot of activities on campus? Do they have movies, concerts, a game room or quiet area to read and study? Will there be some campus functions to attend after a difficult week of studying.

❏ **25. Safety of the campus.** How safe is the campus and surrounding area? Will you be in danger by walking alone at night?

# IV. Athletic Facilities

❏ **26. The locker rooms.** Is it a state-of-the-art setting you long for, or just something common enough to have it's own down-home personality? The main thing is you must have an area to dress, shower and store your personal belongings.

❏ **27. Training room.** This should be a good facility. Does it have up-to-date equipment? Will you easily be able to rehab any kind of injury?

❏ **28. Practice area.** This area doesn't have to be glamorous, but it should be clean and safe.

❏ **29. Game facilities.** How many screaming fans does it hold? Is it different or the same as the practice area?

# V. Athletic Program

❏ **30. Head coach and assistants.** The head coach should be a good communicator and have an open-door policy. If not, then one of the assistants should be able to come to your aid in any problems that may occur. Will you get along with the staff? Please, be objective.

❏ **31. Players on the team.** Remember if you did not meet the other players on the team during your official visit, there's something extremely wrong with the way the coach conducts business. Does the team have a family atmosphere? Do the members talk about winning as a team or individual goals? Are the student-athletes happy? Find out if the coach is fair. It's very important to receive feedback from your potential teammates because some of them will be with you for the majority of your career.

❏ **32. Junior college transfer student-athletes.** How many will be coming in and who will play your position? Junior college student-athletes are usually recruited to play immediately and that could place you on the bench for a year or two.

❏ **33. School's tradition.** How important is the school's athletic program? Does the entire community get involved? Does it have a winning or losing tradition? What is the team's win-loss record over the last ten years or so?

❏ **34. Position you will play in college.** Will the coach change your perceived natural position? Will you be able to make a smooth transition to the college level?

❏ **35. Team's style of play.** If you're a high-paced basketball player, you don't want to play in a slow-it-down system. If you're a drop-back quarterback, you don't want to play in a system that uses the wishbone offense. This is very important to your happiness in college.

❏ **36. Will you play early in your career?** Coaches usually prefer not to hand starting positions to high school student-athletes, but they do from time to time. Some coaches will tell you that a starting spot is yours to lose, while others will grant you the opportunity to earn significant playing time.

❏ **37. Local media.** Some people who cover college athletics tend to fall in love with the team and report with overblown expectations, while others are overly critical. Some remain neutral and cover teams like professional journalists should. Some cover the program so closely that if you're handed a parking ticket, you'll read about it the next morning. Find out which type you will be dealing with.

❏ **38. Schedule.** What's the strength of the school's schedule? Is it a soft schedule? Will you play against high-quality competition?

# VI. Intangibles

❏ **39. Which coach revokes the most scholarships?** Who has the highest turnover rate? Some coaches snatch scholarships if you don't produce athletically, while others take them away because of injury. Make sure you find out why a coach takes away scholarships. Also, if a coach has a high turnover rate each year, it could mean the student-athletes were unhappy with the coach and transferred.

❏ **40. NCAA rules violations**. Has the program ever been investigated or penalized by the NCAA recently? A program on probation could mean one in rebuilding and not invited to postseason play.

Now, carefully, add up the total. The lowest possible score a college can receive is 35 points, the highest is 350. The college with the highest tally should be the one for you.

## Home and Official Visits

The late Jim Valvano once won over the mother of a recruit by speaking perfect Italian during his home visit. When Sonja Hogg was the women's basketball coach at Louisiana Tech, she prided herself on her chameleon-like ability to blend into whatever home environment necessary to land recruits. Often times, that meant going into a recruit's home, sitting down for family dinner and eating various dishes from black eyed peas and corn bread to quiche. Clemson men's basketball coach Rick Barnes dazzles recruits with unconventional magic tricks. These are all carefully planned courses of action that turned recruits on during home visits. However, some coaches can be a tad disrespectful.

On a rainy evening in chilly upstate New York, former University of Michigan football coach Bo Schembechler traveled to the home of a powerful lineman who was wanted by virtually every school in the Big Ten. When Schembechler arrived to the recruit's home, he failed to wipe off his feet at the door and left paths of mud throughout the house.

"If he can't respect my home," bellowed the recruit's father, "he won't respect my kid."

The recruit signed with Purdue University.

Rochelle Boyce said when Kevin O'Neill was the basketball coach at Marquette University, he applied vice-grip like pressure on her son, Donnie, to become a part of the Warriors family, or risk having the scholarship being offered to another recruit. O'Neill's tactics cost Marquette Donnie, a future second-round NBA draft pick, who signed with Colorado.

The best recruiters have the ability to discuss anything from the latest in hip-hop music, to suggestions on redecorating the family recreation room. The right stroke on a home visit could land a coach a ticket to the coveted national spotlight.

It was noted that assistant coaches pilot the bulk of the recruitment of student-athletes, but home visits present the time when the head coach makes his pitch.

But before you allow a recruiter into your home, you should make certain the coach represents a school you want to attend. Ask yourself, has this coach been following my recruiting guidelines? Is the school too far away or too close to home? Does the school offer my intended major? You should promptly eliminate schools which do not meet your criteria. For basketball players, the contact period allowed by the NCAA begins in early September. If you are considering making a commitment during the early signing period in November, you should have a good idea about which coaches will visit by late August or early September. For basketball student-athletes who choose to wait until April, the list should be narrowed down by late January or early February. For football players, contact periods begin in December so the list should be narrowed down by late October or early November.

If you aren't a blue-chip athlete like football's Steve McNair or basketball's Alonzo Mourning, it might be best for you to think about all your options carefully before turning down a home visit from a school. For example, you may be interested in pursuing a law degree. Duke may contend for the national title with or without your help, and maybe you'll see little playing time for four years. Nevertheless, it has the nation's best law school. Clemson is offering you a chance to start immediately, but its law program isn't nearly as flattering. Which school should you attend?

Recruiters are acute salesmen. They will speak of attractive subjects such as their university's $10 million state of the art sports facility, the millions of people they play in front of, how much television exposure they receive, the student apartments, and how tremendous the social environment is. How much recruiters expound on education, the student body, housing and other topics depends on the feedback they receive from you and your parents or guardians. For example, a recruiter probably won't tell you about his team's graduation rate unless it's exceptional. Recruiters won't expand on why they revoke so many scholarships each year unless you confront the coach on the issue.

You need to ask more questions than: How many good teams does your school schedule? How many times are you on television? What kinds of sneakers or spikes does the team wear? You have to be concerned with the school's standing on academics and tutoring programs as well as the campus environment and social life. Some sample questions you can ask during the home visit include, but are not limited to, include:

❑ **1. Information on my intended major.**

- ◼ How does your school rank in the country in my intended major?

- ◼ How many credit hours will I need to graduate?

- ◼ How many credit hours will I need to average per semester to graduate in four or five years?

- ◼ Teacher to student ratio?

- ◼ Information on summer internships or co-op programs.

❏ **2. If I need five years to graduate, will the university be there for me?**

■ If I don't qualify academically as a freshman, will I be accepted to your university?

■ If I sign with your school, can I come to campus before the fall semester?

■ Will you pay for my summer-school education?

■ Contacts for job prospects after graduation.

❏ **3. Tutorial programs.**

■ How often are tutors available for me?

■ Will I be able to use a tape recorder in the classroom?

■ Do you have a study hall program?

■ How long are the practice sessions each day?

■ How long will I be able to study each week?

❏ **4. Player graduation rate.**

■ What percentage of your players graduate in four to five years?

■ How often will the coaches check my progress toward graduation?

❏ **5. How long is your contract?**

■ How long have you been at the university?

■ Is your job in jeopardy?

■ Are you or any of your assistants looking into other coaching opportunities?

■ (For a new coach) How long has the university given you to turn the program around?

■ Has your program ever been investigated by the NCAA and/or placed on probation?

❑ **6. How would you characterize your coaching style?**

- Tell me how I would fit in?

- What types of offenses and defenses are used in your system?

- Will you switch me from my natural position?

- How many professional athletes have you coached?

❑ **7. How competitive is your schedule?**

- Who are some of the top teams you play?

- How often do you play on television?

- How much time will we spend on the road?

❑ **8. Relationship with the players.**

- How many players have left your program during your tenure?

- How many transfer students do you allow into your program each year?

- Will I meet the players during my official visit?

- Can I visit with non-student-athletes during my visit?

- Who else are you recruiting at my position?

- How many scholarships have you revoked during your tenure and why?

At the end of your home visit, a recruiter will usually attempt to set a time for the student-athlete to make an official visit to the campus. An official visit to a university by a student-athlete is financed in whole or in part by the university. Recruiters view a well-orchestrated official visit as the opportunity to close the deal. The primary emphasis of an official visit is to reinforce what you and the coach discussed during the home visit.

Here are some key points you should remember about an official visit:

❑ 1. An NCAA member institution may finance only one visit to its campus for a student-athlete.

❑ 2. A student-athlete and his parents are allowed to make official visits.

❑ 3. A recruit may take a maximum of five expense-paid visits, with no more than one permitted to any single university. This restriction applies regardless of the number of sports in which a student-athlete is involved.

❑ 4. A student-athlete may not be provided a paid official visit earlier than the opening day of classes of the recruit's senior year in high school.

❑ 5. Student-athletes must have an official PSAT, SAT or ACT test score to qualify for an official visit. This doesn't mean a passing score, but an official one.

❑ 6. The visit lasts 48 hours and includes transportation, lodging and meals. Entertainment can be no more than $20 per day.

❑ 7. Student-athletes mostly eat in restaurants and stay in a hotel within a 30-mile radius of the campus.

❑ 8. Student-athletes are permitted to attend a school's athletic event free, but aren't allowed to sit in the press box, a private box or on the bench.

The NCAA has done considerable work cleaning up official visits. The biggest move came in 1987 when boosters were banned from having contact with recruits. Before then, it was common for a USC football recruit to have a nice quiet dinner at O.J. Simpson's house. Limousine and helicopter rides were also the norm at major universities.

High school coaches are divided on if student-athlete's should take the five visits allowed by the NCAA. It actually depends on the stature of the student-athlete.

A player with Steve McNair-like ability can probably take five visits without worrying about the school offering the scholarship to another prospect. A student-athlete with good, but not great ability, may not be so lucky.

Before his official visit to the University of Washington in 1993, quarterback Brady Batten from Bakersfield, California narrowed his choices down to the University of Arizona and Washington. After his Washington trip, Batten remained undecided and wanted to take his trip to Arizona.

"I asked the coaches at Washington, 'If I wanna sign right now, can I sign?'" Batten said. "They said, 'Yeah, the scholarship is there for you right now.'"

Batten informed the Washington staff that he wanted to return home and think about it. "I told them I was going to make a decision between them and Arizona," he said. "They said, 'Okay, that should be fine. Don't feel rushed or anything.'"

Batten returned home and was shocked to learn the Huskies received verbal commitments from two other quarterback prospects the day after his Washington official visit. Washington no longer needed Batten. He signed with Arizona.

The decision on whether you should take all official visits is almost as difficult as selecting a school to attend. You should seek advice from parents and coaches on how to approach this situation. When talking to a recruiter, you should ask him to be honest about if the scholarship will be available after taking all your official visits.

Here are a few things you should consider before taking an official visit:

❏ 1. You should not plan a trip to a school you have no intention of attending. A free trip to the University of Hawaii or Miami would be nice, but not if you are wasting the recruiter's time.

❑ 2. When you arrive on campus, you should make certain to take in all it has to offer. If you are interested in student government, the student newspaper or social life, you should make sure to see all of them.

❑ 3. You should take the trip when you will miss a minimum amount of classwork. Why miss a biology exam when you can take a recruiting trip the following weekend?

❑ 4. Make certain you are able to meet all potential teammates. Coaches who do not allow you to meet with members of the team may have something to hide and the player should not get involved with a potentially uncomfortable situation.

❑ 5. Request some time with regular students who are not associated with the athletic department. Receiving feedback from these students will help you decide if the school is right for you.

❑ 6. Spend some time in the dormitories. The NCAA has disallowed "athletic dorms" because there was a theory that the athletes were isolated from the general student body. Spend some time in student housing to see how comfortable it is.

❑ 7. Request some time to meet with a professor from the department of your intended major and sit in on a classroom setting. By talking to a professor you should discover if you will be comfortable in the classroom.

"Whatever it is you're looking for, you need to list them and figure out where the best place to get those things is," said former UNLV men's basketball assistant coach Mark Warkentein.

If a school visits your home and invites you for an official visit, it is likely that university will offer you a scholarship. Nevertheless, that's not the way college recruiters made Donnie Boyce and his mother, Rochelle, feel.

Recruiters who didn't know any better expected Donnie to be another raw, adroit athlete with a questionable jump shot. An athlete in the tradition of Chicago Bulls star Scottie Pippen, save a few inches. But if recruiters had taken a longer glance at Donnie's resume, they would have discovered that by the fall of his senior year in high school he had just turned 17. There was much room for growth, much room for maturation.

His mother grew up deep on Chicago's South Side, where the bass throughout the rhythm of the sport thumped hard and loud. The city's hard edge never sank deeply into Donnie because he grew up in suburban Maywood, Ill., but he somehow clutched the megalopolis game.

Donnie was regarded as one of the nation's top 100 prospects in 1990, but was the third best player on his Proviso East High School team behind Sherell Ford, who signed with the University of Illinois-Chicago, and Michael Finley who selected the University of Wisconsin. Because of his more heralded teammates, Boyce never heard the hosannas of recruiters. Donnie, a 6-5 swingman, was the more versatile of the trio and his cool demeanor earned him the moniker "Sleepy." Donnie averaged 12.8 points and 10.5 rebounds after embarking on a heartbreaking recruiting process which left him thinking he wasn't going to be able to attend the school of his choice.

Donnie signed with the University of Colorado during the early signing period in November 1990, but it wasn't his first choice. His first instinct was to select DePaul University in Chicago, although his mother wanted him to get away from home and attend Marquette University in Milwaukee. Initially, Rochelle, a single parent since Donnie's freshman year at Proviso East, was a mere neophyte to the recruiting process. After several conversations between the Boyces and Bill Hitt, then the boys basketball coach at Proviso East, the Boyces set up home visits with Colorado, DePaul, Marquette, USC, and Florida.

"The most hectic part for us was having the coaches come in," Rochelle said. "It was quite scary. They really tried to butter you up. They didn't come out and say Donnie would be starting, but the impression you would have gotten is he was going to start."

Marquette appeared to have a slight edge over the other four schools early in the recruitment of Donnie. Warriors assistant coach Bo Ellis, who led Marquette to the 1977 national championship as a player, was friends with some people Rochelle grew up with in Chicago. Rochelle says Marquette coach Kevin O'Neill attempted to use Ellis' association with the Boyce family to influence Donnie to signing with Marquette, but when the Boyces indicated they wanted to explore other options O'Neill's attitude became icy. During Donnie's home visit, the assertive O'Neill, who carved his niche as a crafty recruiter as an assistant at Arizona, threw his inflexible pitch.

"When we met, I wasn't impressed with coach O'Neill," Rochelle said. "He wanted us to make a decision that day and it was like, if we didn't make a decision, 'don't worry about it, we're not coming back.' He didn't (exactly) say those words, but that's the way he left us."

Puzzled by O'Neill's remarks, Donnie informed him again he wanted to take other official visits. If Marquette wanted him, Donnie thought, they would be there for him after he completed his visits. He quickly sent up an official visit with his dream school—DePaul.

As a youngster, Donnie was an avid admirer of the Blue Demons program because of their freewheeling style, rich basketball tradition and coach Joey Meyer. He was in awe watching former Blue Demon stars Mark Aquirre, Terry Cummings and Rod Strickland. Nevertheless, Meyer was hot after prep All-Americans Tom Kleinschmidt of Chicago and Howard Nathan from downstate Peoria, Illinois.

For nearly a decade, the Blue Demons were having difficulty keeping the top talent in Chicago and the signing of Kleinschmidt, a gritty 6-5 swingman with a silky jump shot, would help ease that barren reputation. Nathan was a pure lead guard in the mold of Isiah Thomas with the ability to drain a few jumpers from beyond the three-point arch. Kleinschmidt will finish his career at DePaul as one of the finest ever, but Nathan's stay was merely a stopover after he was declared academically ineligible following his freshman season. He later transferred to Northeast Louisiana University after a year at a junior college.

When Donnie made his official visit to the DePaul, he was treated indifferent at best by the Blue Demons' coaching staff. "They seemed to be more interested in Kleinschmidt and Nathan," he said. "They had the bigger names coming out of high school than me."

Unlike O'Neill, Meyer didn't tell Donnie he needed a verbal commitment from him after the visit or the scholarship would be given to another player. Donnie informed Meyer that he wanted to take his visit to Colorado before making a decision. But the week following his DePaul visit, Donnie learned how the recruiting game is truly played.

O'Neill received a verbal commitment from William Gates, a 6-foot defender deluxe from nearby St. Joseph's High School in Westchester. Because of his superior vertical leaping ability, Gates was comfortable playing point guard, shooting guard or small forward. Donnie was no longer wanted by the Warriors.

"That showed me they didn't have a true interest in me," Donnie said.

Kleinschmidt and Nathan both committed to the Blue Demons, instantly elevating DePaul to the top of the recruiting charts. The Blue Demons told Donnie no, thank you. Both hits occurred on the same day for the Boyces.

Donnie attempted set up official visits with USC and Florida, the other two schools who expressed interest, but both also received commitments from other student-athletes who played similar positions.

"Everything went to pieces after the home visits," Donnie said. "I was supposed to make some visits, but the schools would sign someone else first. (I realized) they were going to take the first guy that they could. They were telling me, 'You could fit in our program real nice.' They were just lying to get what they wanted. I was thinking I wasn't going to play at a high Division I school and I'd have to settle for a mid-major Division I school," Donnie said.

Donnie began to consider the University of Loyola-Chicago, the University of Illinois-Chicago, Illinois State University and other schools in the Mid-Continent Conference. "Those aren't bad schools but I was looking for something higher," Donnie said.

The Boyces' only misdeed was being patient and thorough. Rochelle wanted Donnie to take his time, comb through what the recruiters had to offer, then make a decision. It would have been extremely difficult for Rochelle to pay for Donnie to attend a school such as DePaul or Marquette, and Donnie questioned his decision to take other official visits. Also, Boyce wanted to sign in November, concentrate on his school work, and lead Proviso East to the state championship which he did. Winning the state title was probably easier. He didn't want to wait until April, and his head was spinning. *Take all your visits. Check out all the options. Did we do the right thing?*

"I was very upset with them (DePaul and Marquette)," Rochelle said. "If I had said, 'Donnie, forget about the other visits and sign with DePaul,' everything would have been okay, but I didn't think that's the way it should have been done. You're supposed to have a number of choices and then you make a choice. I didn't get the impression we were going to be forced into anything from Joey Meyer, but I did get that from O'Neill. I wanted him to go to Marquette. He would have a chance to be away from home. He would have been far enough away but close to home. I liked DePaul, but I thought he would have been too close to home and he wouldn't have that experience of being away for college. He felt like he wasn't going to get chosen. Then Marquette picked that guy from Saint Joe's, and DePaul turned around and did the same thing...it was a terrible week."

There was only one major Division I school remaining—Colorado.

Donnie made his official visit to Colorado a week before the November early signing period of 1990. Buffaloes coach Joe Harrington was the only coach who didn't pressure Donnie into giving him an oral commitment. Colorado instantly granted Rochelle's wish of her son attending a school away from Chicago, and pacified Donnie's thirst for playing at a major Division I school. Colorado was noted more for its high-powered football program which wrestled a share of the national title that year, but Donnie would be able to bump heads with high quality Big Eight competition. Colorado was beginning to look better and better.

"I really had fun," said Donnie of his official visit to Colorado. "It was the place that showed the most interest in me and was fair about it. Even if I didn't sign in the fall, they would have been waiting on me in the spring."

The Colorado players made Donnie feel welcome by taking him to a campus party during his official visit, then sitting and talking the rest of the time. "It was like being at home," he said. "They never acted like they didn't want me there and I was just another recruit."

Marquette, DePaul and the others lost out on a player who poured in nearly 1,000 points after two seasons. Only two other players have scored more points after two seasons in the storied history of Big Eight basketball—Oklahoma's Wayman Tisdale and Kansas' Danny Manning, and both were NBA first-round draft picks. But at times, Donnie's decision to attend Colorado has been questioned by many...including himself.

Donnie thought about leaving the program after the 1992-93 season upon assistant coach Tom Abatemarco's departure to Rutgers University. He was very close to Abatemarco. Rumors were flying that Donnie was headed to Michigan, Wisconsin and even Marquette, but he decided to remain at Colorado. There was friction between Boyce and Harrington during the 1992-93 season and it boiled over during a home loss to Oklahoma State. Boyce reportedly spent much of the second half of that game aloof on the court, relaxing on offense. Boyce, who led the Buffaloes in scoring with 19.1 points per game, finished with three points. A rankled Harrington benched Boyce and refused to start him the next game against Iowa State.

Losing hasn't been easy for Donnie, either. During his first three years at the school, CU was 33-59. In Donnie's three years of playing varsity at Proviso East, the Pirates finished with a 99-19 mark, capturing a state championship and a No. 6 ranking by *USA Today* following the 1990 season.

"He wanted to know if he was going into the right direction," Rochelle said. "With coach Tom leaving, it kind of made him wonder, and he looked at other options. He's doing very well in the Big Eight, but it's just so far away."

The way time telescopes, it seems like millions of years ago but the sting of the recruiting process remains inside the Boyces. Looking back, they would have done everything differently. Instead of signing in November, Rochelle says Donnie would have waited and signed during the late signing period in April. Donnie says he would have committed to DePaul.

"I would have told them after I visited, 'Yeah, I want to come here,' instead of trying to take some more visits. That's the only thing I would have done differently. I didn't tell them I wanted to come, but I wanted to visit more schools," he said.

"If they (recruiters) don't think your potential is up to par, they tell you, 'Yeah, we really want you,' but as soon they find someone who they think is better, they'll sign them in a minute and forget about you."

Donnie Boyce no longer needs two forms of identification for coaches to recognize him. He finished his career at Colorado as the school's career scoring leader and was drafted in the second-round by the Atlanta Hawks in 1995. He will go down in Colorado history as one of the school's finest athletes ever—in any sport. But he nearly had to attend a school beneath his playing ability.

"I didn't think he'd be that good," one Midwestern coach admitted. "We'd take him right now and we're loaded at guard...but he's Donnie Boyce."

Did Donnie make the right decision by waiting and gathering all the information? In hindsight, Donnie was a success at Colorado and was drafted into the NBA, but he attended a school he really didn't want to go to.

The fact is, none of us should be forced to make hasty decisions that affect the rest of our lives.

Notes:

# Chapter 7

## Who should Handle Your Recruiting?

Ralph is a former assistant coach who, for the time being, is fed up with the dirty dealings which dwell in college basketball. He insisted on remaining anonymous because his love for the game may lure him back into coaching, and there are some bridges he does not want to burn.

Ralph got his first opportunity coaching on the Division I level in 1984, and successfully recruited one of the Chicago area's top point guards the following year. Because the recruitment of this student-athlete was smooth and above board, Ralph felt he had the makings of a positive pipeline into the talent-rich Windy City, which boasts an average of 40 to 60 NCAA Division I basketball prospects each winter. Assistant coaches have come to realize that successful recruiting in Chicago is a fast track to a desired head-coaching position. Chicago-area high-school coaches realize this as well.

Ralph was sitting in a gym during the summer of 1985 when he noticed the high-school coach of one of the best programs in the Chicago area strolled in. Ralph wanted to get the telephone number of the coach's top player so he introduced himself and handed the coach a media guide from his university. Then, Ralph was smacked with a large dose of recruiting reality.

"He said that I was going to have to let his kids go to our summer camp for free and then we were going to have to send him some gym shoes," Ralph said. "It was my second year and I thought, 'Well that's kind of strange.' I told him. I don't know how we could do that. We're 1,500 miles away and we're not going to be able to bring your kids to summer camp. We don't have enough shoes for our own kids. He was real short with me and I haven't talked to him since."

The coach was handling the recruiting for his player, yet obviously didn't have the best interest of the student-athlete. What he asked Ralph to do is against NCAA rules. Do you want a person like this handling your recruiting? A person who would sellout a student-athlete to a school for a pair of gym shoes and free passes to a summer basketball camp?

"That's the way it is with some people when it comes to recruiting," Ralph said. "Some people who handle a kid's recruitment, want to go on an ego trip. They want the money and the glory and some college recruiters will hand it to them. It's just business."

Just business.

More and more you hear curious tales about how middlemen are attempting to muscle their way into the potentially profitable world of recruiting. Middlemen, or street agents, as they are commonly called, are playing a significant role in where certain student-athletes attend college.

Inner-city athletes from single-parent environments tend to fall prey to these wastrel street agents. They spot a talented youngster early, buy them clothes, sneakers, food, take them to movies, give them money and in some cases make life easier for college recruiters. Slowly they gain the youngster's sympathetic trust. Because these street agents aren't the student-athlete's parent or guardian, the NCAA does not have the power to limit the number of contacts college recruiters may have with them.

Ask any recruiter and they will tell you they don't like dealing with street agents. Nevertheless, a street agent is in the way of the college recruiter's prize—the student-athlete. If a street agent can assist in gaining information on an athlete, which in turn will lead to the prize, so be it. *Which camps will the student-athlete be attending during the evaluation period? Who's the student-athlete's favorite college coach? Which schools do they like? How can we move up?* The street agent knows or can find out. Nevertheless, the use of a talent scout to recruit players is forbidden by the NCAA.

"It's gotten outrageous because now you have AAU coaches, summer league coaches, high school coaches and then you have the parents," says Tracy Dildy, an assistant men's basketball coach at DePaul University. "It's a case where you have to go through so many people, and I don't agree with it at all. I like to go through the parents, and while I think the coach should be involved, I don't think the coach has the right to make the decision (on which college the student-athlete should attend). Nine out of 10 times the AAU coach or the summer league coach is making the decision."

Which is what some say happened to former Syracuse University basketball player Tony Scott in 1990. Scott is one of the better players to pass through East High School in Rochester, New York, and before he began his freshman season at the Big East school in 1988, Syracuse assistant coach Bernie Fine felt he possessed the offensive potential to someday play in the NBA. But in two years at Syracuse, Scott never really caught the tempo of the physical, brawl-for-it-all mode of the Big East conference. Scott was rail-thin youngster, sorely lacking in the fundamentals of the game. He wanted and needed to transfer to another school. That's when New York talent scout Rob Johnson stepped in.

Scott told *The Post-Standard* of Syracuse in 1990 that he transferred to Texas A&M University in a deal brokered by Johnson. Scott told the newspaper that A&M coach Kermit Davis, Jr., who was later fired from the school after an NCAA investigation, had promised extra benefits to him, his family and Johnson. Johnson allegedly told Scott he received $2,400 to work two weeks at Davis' summer camp at A&M.

"I thought he was a friend of mine," Scott, told *The Post-Standard* "It turns out that he sold me to this program."

The day after the Scott story broke in Syracuse, former East High coach Sal Rizzo told the *Times-Union* in Rochester that someone demanded A&M pay Scott "a ridiculous sum" of money after Scott transferred to the College Station, Texas school. Rizzo said two days after Scott signed a National Letter of Intent with the Aggies, he received a telephone call from a man claiming to be an A&M assistant who said he couldn't give Scott the money.

"He said, 'We can't give him $20,000,' or whatever ridiculous sum it was," Rizzo told the *Times-Union*. "I said, 'Who said you had to?' He said this guy came down with Tony and said we have to give him some money so he can live. I told him, 'You know the NCAA rules better than I do. Do what you have to.'"

Scott later recanted the story which included more minor NCAA infractions, and told family and friends he committed an enormous error by leaving the Orangemen program. Scott left A&M in disgrace just months after the story broke, and never played another minute of college basketball.

"I called some schools like Canisius and St. Bonaventure, but they didn't want him," Rizzo said. "Nobody wanted Tony."

People soon forgot that before his senior year of high school, Scott made a verbal commitment to attend the University of Connecticut. Would things have been different if he hadn't reneged on his commitment? Did Scott make a mistake by dealing with Rob Johnson?

You have to find someone you can trust to handle the recruiting. That person has to be someone who will not accept offers or inducements from college recruiters, which are against NCAA regulations. Accepting inducements from college recruiters can put your eligibility in jeopardy.

Another option for the student-athlete and parent is to handle the recruiting themselves and establish guidelines for recruiters. Tacoma, Washington's Kate Starbird, an excellent student-athlete, orchestrated her own recruiting and decided on Stanford University.

"I pretty much did everything myself," said Starbird, an All-American from Lakes High School. "I set up times when recruiters could call and they followed those times. For the most part, it wasn't a big deal."

Starbird finished her four-year career at Stanford as an All-American and signed a lucrative contract to play professionally in the American Basketball League (ABL).

If you know of someone who has the reputation for being a street agent and that person wants to "represent" you, perhaps you should consider another alternative. If the person remains persistent, you should inform your parents, guardian, coach, and contact the NCAA.

Let's take a look at how two former high school coaches handled the recruitment of their youngsters.

✷ ✷ ✷ ✷ ✷

When Pat Mancuso stepped down as football coach at Princeton High School in 1996, he finished with over 40 seasons of coaching experience, including over 300 wins. During the last decade when Princeton emerged from being a top-drawer local team to one of national prominence, Mancuso sent an average of 8-10 players per season to the collegiate level. Recruiting was an on-going process for Mancuso and his coaching staff at Princeton. They never had an off-season.

"We go at it all year in the sense of making them (the players) aware when the ACT and SAT and PSAT's are," he said. "We constantly advise the parents of the status of their youngster's GPA. We send letters home to the parents to that effect. We keep the kids abreast of the rules and regulations of recruiting, so it's a never-ending thing for us."

By April, Mancuso and an assistant would list all his seniors-to-be, Division I prospects or not, for evaluation. They obtained the student-athlete's GPA, test scores, height, weight and college potential. Then Mancuso and Knepshield would confer about which level was suitable for the youngster. Some student-athletes would emerge as Division I prospects by the fall, while others would slip a notch. Then Mancuso mails the list, "to damn near every college in the country," he said. When recruiters came to the Princeton campus to begin their evaluation period in May, Mancuso's list was in hand.

"They come in and say, 'We're interested in so and so, and so and so,' or 'this kid looks good, but he's not tall enough,'" Mancuso said. "We get a good response from them."

After the college recruiters completed their assessments, Mancuso took a hands-off approach and allowed the parents and student-athletes to deal with the myriad of phone calls. He also encouraged the players and parents to set up recruiting visits. The parents and student-athletes were well versed on the recruiting process by Mancuso, but if at any time they felt uncomfortable with handling the recruiting, he was willing to give counsel when needed. Because Mancuso educated the parents and student-athletes about the recruiting process, Princeton wasn't affected by street agents.

"I never, and I don't say 'never' often, tell a kid where he should go," Mancuso said. "I think that's up to the parents. It's our responsibility to get that athlete the opportunity to go where he might want to go if he has the ability. But it's the parents and his responsibility to select the right school."

\* \* \* \* \*

Coach Norwaine Reed claimed he only needed three talented players to have a winning team. Coaching basketball, in his opinion, was rather rudimentary. A quick glance at Reed's recruiting track record at Buena Vista High School conveys he coached more than a few good players during his tenure. Reed, the coach at the Saginaw, Michigan school from 1983-95, sent nearly 100 players to the collegiate level.

"Not all of these kids go on (athletic) scholarships," Reed said. "Some of those kids who we helped get into school were academic people. In the last 10 years, we've had three valedictorians. We had one finish up at (the University of) Michigan and now he's in the business world in Chicago. These players weren't just filling up a uniform, they were significant players who we helped get into college."

Reed had a special program called Competitive Edge to Peak Performance at his high school. There is almost year-round work on the essential aspects of basketball, and Reed also had his student-athletes keep a daily journal. There was a great emphasis on visual techniques, with imagining eventual success and attitude reinforcement.

Reed approached the recruiting process differently than most. He recruits the college for the student-athlete, not vice-versa. Reed, the student-athlete, and the parents or guardian set up criteria for schools. They focused on subjects like type of major, tutors, and financial aid. Reed worked earnestly to find the right school for the youngster. He made certain that his student-athlete is academically eligible to play "any place where the athlete could get his education." He spent hundreds of hours and his own money on the telephone calling schools and conducting research at the library trying to find the right match. Reed didn't seek hand-outs for his players, just the opportunity to work and earn a priceless education.

Many coaches called Reed for information on his players and he simply listened to their presentations and jotted down notes. It's a process he didn't particularly care for because he doesn't like the way some recruiters conducted business.

Some college recruiters gave the impression that they are doing him a favor by recruiting his players, Reed says.

"It's an honor to be recruited, but I don't think a college should make you feel at the mercy of any college," he says. "They (the student-athlete) shouldn't feel in awe. I could care less whether recruiters come around or not."

Reed didn't have an open-door policy when it came to recruiting his players, and if college coaches tried to come through the backdoor, he was there to quickly escort them out through the front. Recruiters are prohibited from watching Reed's players in an open-gym atmosphere without his permission. He isn't an egomaniac, so Reed doesn't need to be stroked. "(Some) high school coaches, because of the recruiting process, end up running plantation markets for these college coaches," he said.

The first player who went through Reed's process was former Detroit Pistons guard Mark Macon, who graduated from Buena Vista in 1987 and signed with Temple University in Philadelphia. Macon was a high school All-American, MVP of the prestigious McDonald's All-American Game, and Mr. Basketball in the state of Michigan. He was Reed's first major star pupil, and he wanted to keep the recruiting from getting out of hand. Macon made the process easier on Reed by making it clear he wanted to play for an African-American coach in college.

Reed made numerous telephone calls to coaches all over the country marketing his 6-foot-5 player, who happened to be one of the best shooting guards in the nation. Macon decided on Temple because the Owls' coach, John Chaney, and Reed share similar philosophies— discipline and hard work will eventually lead to rewards. Georgetown University, and its coach, John Thompson, was Macon's second choice.

For Reeds' daughter, Erinn, the process of searching for a college began when she was 12 years old. By the time she was prepared to enter high school, Erinn knew she would become a major Division I prospect, and selected the University of Iowa in 1993.

"Michigan sent me my first letter when I was in the fifth grade," said Erinn, a first-team *USA Today* All-American selection as a senior in 1993. "At the time, I didn't think about it. I was in elementary school and I just wanted to play basketball. I didn't think about college, I guess I had a one-track mind."

When Erinn reached junior high school, she was receiving letters on a regular basis which were closely monitored by her father. The total grew to 3,000 from 80 universities prior to Erinn signing with Iowa. Erinn and her father began fielding calls on July 1 prior to her senior year, which is the first day the NCAA allows student-athletes to receive calls from recruiter. They were curt and to the point with schools she wasn't interested in. By late August, Erinn selected the colleges she was going to visit.

Erinn realized as a junior which school she wanted to attend—Iowa. Norwaine, however, insisted on Erinn making the five official visits allowed by the NCAA. If Kansas, for example, was a better school for Erinn, Norwaine didn't want Erinn to miss out on the opportunity. The Reed's developed the following criteria:

1. A good education curriculum, Erinn's intended major.

2. A coach with a winning record.

3. A coach who had a good rapport with the players.

4. A winning program with an opportunity to win a national championship.

5. Team unity.

6. A friendly campus atmosphere.

Erinn's final five selections were Texas, Kansas, Penn State, Virginia, and Iowa. "I thought they were very great programs," Norwaine said. "For Erinn, they (the schools) were really geared to giving equal opportunities to women. They didn't take a back seat to any of the men's programs, and that's what we were looking for."

Erinn found out about Virginia while attending a camp at Iowa when coach Debbie Ryan was a guest speaker. Erinn didn't know much about Penn State, but Norwaine is friends with Dan Durkin, a former assistant who later became coach at Duquesne University. Texas' reputation as a party school caught Erinn's attention, as well as commanding coach Jody Conradt and two-time Naismith Trophy winner Clarissa

Davis, a former Longhorn All-American. Kansas entered the picture at the last minute, and Erinn was taken by coach Marian Washington's standing as a relentless recruiter. Erinn was going to visit either Michigan or Michigan State for her fifth and final official visit, until Washington flashed her winning resume. Erinn soon discovered All-American Lynette Woodard blossomed under Washington at Kansas.

So Erinn went through the recruiting process, part of an ongoing learning experience that would help her later in life, Norwaine told her. But she knew what she wanted all along. She wanted Iowa.

Iowa had one of the nation's top programs in education, and not only did coach Vivian Stringer lead the Hawkeyes to the Final Four in 1993, but she had the reputation as one of the true motivators and communicators in all of college basketball. But Iowa won Erinn's heart, and perhaps the nation's top point guard, with it's friendly surroundings. Iowa embraces everyone—athletes, students, professionals, janitors and the local barber—into the Hawkeye family.

"At any other place, if you don't know anyone, you're a stranger," Erinn said. "But at Iowa it's different. People will see you and if they don't know you they'll say, 'Hi, how are you doing?' Everybody seems happy and everyone is smiling at each other. They call it 'User Friendly.'"

"The coaches are always concerned about you and its a very relaxed atmosphere. At the other schools I visited, it was business only and the coach was never really around the players. After practice or after the game, the players are on their own. At Iowa, the coaches like being around the players like one big family."

It also helped that Erinn attended Stringer's camps each summer since the age of 12, and became close friends with the esteemed coach. "Vivian knows the game backwards and forwards," Norwaine said.

So the anxiety that some heavily recruited student-athletes feel was not matched by the young lady who one college coach said is like watching a pocket-sized Joe Dumars. No, Norwaine would have none of that. Anxiety overwhelms an individual when a person can't control the situation.

"What high school coaches have to think about is doing a tremendous amount of research when you talk about a college," Reed said. "It's not always a place where the youngster can be out on the floor quicker, either. Erinn will grow up to earn everything she gets because she doesn't expect people to give her anything."

"Going to Iowa," says Erinn, "is the best decision I've ever made."

Unfortunately for Erinn, Iowa wasn't the best place for her talents. After an uneven freshman season, Erinn transferred to Kansas and two years after Erinn signed with Iowa, Stringer was implementing her User Friendly role at Rutgers University.

## Things to remember when recruiters come calling

❏ 1. In all sports except football, telephone calls from coaches are not permitted by the NCAA until July 1 after completion of your junior year. In football, phone calls from coaches are not permitted until on or after August 15 after the completion of your junior year.

❏ 2. An NCAA college coach is limited to one telephone call per week to the student-athlete.

❏ 3. Monitor your calls. If the calls get out of hand, restrict them to a time you feel comfortable with.

Washington Wizards basketball star Juwan Howard had his high school coach field all his calls from recruiters as a senior at Chicago Vocational.

Howard, who was considered an All-American player before graduating in 1991, made the move to concentrate more in the classroom. He later signed with the University of Michigan and blossomed into a star.

"It was getting too hectic for me and it was just a smart thing to do," he said. "I was getting so many calls that I wasn't getting my homework done. It became so much easier for me to concentrate on my senior year."

The most important thing to remember is to make the recruiting process as comfortable for you as possible. Create a criteria for recruiters to follow and things should run smoothly.

*Photo by Fred Joe*

*Photo by Fred Joe*

*Photo by Lou Kit Wong*

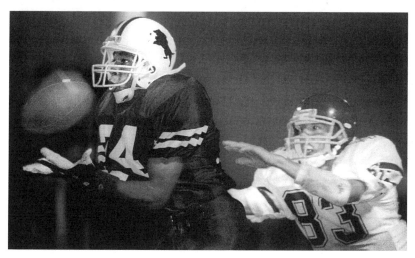

*Photo by Fred Joe*

*Photo by Lou Kit Wong*

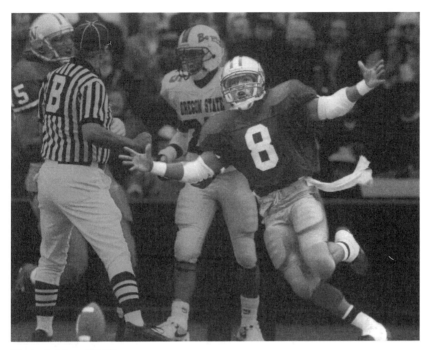

Photo by Lou Kit Wong

Photo by Fred Joe

*Photos by Fred Joe*

Photo by Fred Joe

Notes:

# Chapter 8

## Talent Scouts

Letters from college recruiters tend to generate excitement for the student-athlete. Ninety-nine percent of the time, they don't mean much at all. The cold hard fact is just because you receive letters, doesn't mean you're a lock to receive a scholarship. I remember a young man who received at least 30 letters from major colleges to play basketball, but was never offered a scholarship of any kind following his senior year.

Players receive recruiting letters because they are probably on a long list of prospective student-athletes from numerous scouting services. Some recruiters use scouting services as a supplement to their own intensive work, but coaches never know when they will uncover a sleeper, so they tend to write to nearly everyone on their lists. Let's examine some of high school football's talent scouts.

Tom Lemming from Illinois is perhaps the most respected. This is due in part to the many hours he logs in his car racing across the country to observe talent and the video tapes he collects on student-athletes. Lemming's *Prep Football Report* is well written in a neatly typed package.

*The National Recruiting Advisor* published by Ken Greenberg with managing editor Bobby Burton has deep pockets and calls recruits all over the country to find out where they are thinking about attending school. Greenberg and Burton offer a comprehensive report.

Jeff Duva of *PrepStar* in Woodland Hills, California, was once a quarterback at the University of Hawaii, as well as a college assistant coach. His knowledge of college prospects is unquestioned. Other football scouts include Bill Buchalter, a columnist for *The Orlando Sentinel* in Orlando, Florida who publishes the *Bill Buchalter Recruiting Newsletter*, and Phil Grosz, publisher of Sanatoga, PA-based *G&W Recruiting*.

In boys basketball, Bob Gibbons of Lenior, North Carolina, has long been considered the most respected in the business. Gibbons, the editor of *All Star Sports Publications*, is the selection-committee chairman of the Nike All-American Basketball Festival, and an advisory-committee member of the McDonald's All-American High School Basketball Game.

Tom Konchalski, also a member of the McDonald's advisory committee, is the author of *High School Basketball Illustrated Report* in New York City. The low-key Konchalski has never rated a player he has not seen play. Others include Dave Bones of *Cage Scope*, Van Coleman of *Basketball Times' Future Stars* and Clark Francis of *Hoop Scoop*.

Mike Flynn of Philadelphia has a strong presence in girls basketball, as does Joseph C. Smith, director of Women's Basketball News Service in Corona/Elmhurst, New York.

For the most part, college recruiters and scouts are very thorough when it comes to locating budding talent. For example, Trajan Langdon, a 6-foot-4 basketball player from Anchorage, Alaska, who signed with Duke University in the fall of 1994, was invited to the Nike Festival in the summer of '93. Entering his junior season in 1997, Langdon is one of the nation's top shooters and a strong candidate for All-American honors. Yet some stars go virtually unnoticed early in their careers.

Vin Baker of Hartford University was drafted by the Milwaukee Bucks in the first round of the 1993 NBA Draft. Baker entered Hartford as a freshman with as much flash as a museum guard. He was a 6-7 lightly recruited forward who looked as though he needed a nice square meal, not a Division I scholarship. Only three Division I schools—Hartford,

Rhode Island and Northeastern showed interest in Baker. He grew another three inches and developed his multifaceted skills well enough to play power forward in the NBA. Professional scouts now compare Baker to Chicago Bulls superstar Scottie Pippen, another late bloomer who played at the University of Central Arkansas, a tiny NAIA school in Conway, Arkansas.

As a 5-9 senior with pencil-thin legs, Pippen initially was offered only a scholarship as the water boy for the basketball team at Central Arkansas. He later grew to his current height of 6-7, and helped lead the Bulls to five World Championships.

Nevertheless, it is as easy to overrate talent as it is to underrate it. Former University of Louisville basketball player Tony Kimbro was recognized in the ninth grade as a national-level player. He was profiled in the *Blue Ribbon College Basketball Yearbook,* a respected annual magazine for avid hoops followers, as one of the top 33 players in the country as a high-school sophomore in 1982-83. At 6-7, Kimbro's ability appeared flawless. While his natural position was small forward, he had the adeptness to swing to the backcourt. Kimbro's manner was so placid, he made the game appear rather primitive. He was part of coach Denny Crum's recruiting class which included Pervis Ellison and Kenny Payne, both first-round selections in the 1989 NBA Draft. Kimbro, according to the majority of the talent scouts, was the more gifted of the trio.

Kimbro greeted college basketball with a lasting impression as a freshman during Louisville's national championship run during the 1985-86 season. But his play as a sophomore, along with the entire Cardinals team, was greeted with mixed reviews, as Louisville failed to qualify for the NCAA tournament. He sat out the 1987-88 season for academic reasons, but when he returned to the squad for his final two seasons, he was tagged a major underachiever. For his career, Kimbro averaged 7.9 points and 4.1 rebounds. He shot a respectable 47.1 percent from the field, but these are hardly smashing numbers from a player who was touted as the best all-around player ever produced out of the Louisville prep ranks.

Meanwhile Keith Williams, a teammate of Kimbro's at Seneca High School, also attended Louisville. Williams wasn't as heavily recruited as Kimbro but carved out a better college career, averaging 8.2 points and 3.8 assists. No, these aren't eye-popping statistics but Williams was a sharp-witted player who made good decisions at a point guard and rarely committed mistakes.

Did Kimbro get caught up in being highly regarded at such a tender age that he didn't continue to work on his game? Or, did every scout in the nation merely overestimate the young man's ability?

The following is some of what the 1990-91 *Blue Ribbon College Basketball Yearbook* wrote about Kimbro following his senior year at Louisville:

> "His college career proves that way too much is made of the talent of extremely gifted young players and the result is they often lose their incentive and never develop to the fullest...Many thought he would be the best to ever come out of Louisville...Kimbro basically improved little, if any at all, from the time he was a sophomore in high school until the end of his college career."

Here's what the magazine printed in its 1982-83 edition about Kimbro:

> "Showed strong skills in every area of the game...is versatile enough to have even played some point guard...to be truthful, we had mixed emotions about giving Kimbro this type of exposure...we hate to give a kid a bad reputation so early but it is a fact that he has been in and out of several schools and left his Shawnee team last year...Kimbro is the best sophomore in the country but we hope all of this does not go to his head...his basketball will take care of itself and he needs to concentrate on school work and listening to his teachers and coaches...Kimbro is either going to be a legitimate superstar or wake up and find that the world has passed him by...we certainly hope this exposure has not hampered his

development...hopefully, he will realize that people are now watching him closely and it is time to get prepared for the future."

The first-team high-school selections for *Blue Ribbon* that year included Mark Cline, Antoine Joubert, Tom Sheehey, Dwayne "Pearl" Washington and Reggie Williams. Of those five players, only Williams enjoyed a solid college and NBA career, and he bounced around the league for a few seasons before finding his niche with the Denver Nuggets. As a high school junior, Williams was compared to NBA legend George Gervin.

"I think there's danger in recruiting and the lower you go in age, there's more danger," said Barry Temkin, a *Chicago Tribune* high school sports reporter. "A lot of the time these stars don't turn out to be that good."

Consider Jaron Rush, a 6-7 forward from Kansas City's Pembroke Hill High, who perhaps has more skills than any player from the Class of '98. Last fall, Rush announced he would sign a National Letter of Intent to attend Kansas. Then the youngster had second thoughts primarily, according to *Sports Illustrated*, because Rush felt that Jayhawks coach Roy Williams substituted his players too frequently for his liking.

Later Williams announced that Kansas, a school which has produced noted All-Americans such as Wilt Chamberlain, Danny Manning and Paul Pierce, was no longer recruiting Rush. Rush later announced he would attend UCLA.

"Up until the last couple of years I've enjoyed recruiting," Williams told SI. "I don't enjoy it in 99.9 percent of the cases now. It's always been hard. Now it's gotten to be demeaning."

According to *Sports Illustrated*, Rush's AAU team is bankrolled by millionaire Tom Grant and that Rush drives a $17,000 1995 Geo Tracker that is leased to Grant. According to another basketball publication, *Basketball Times*, Rush has traveled the world, including trips to the Cayman Islands. Yet the consensus of talent scouts throughout the nation is that Rush didn't play up to his potential during the summer of '97, the time when college recruiters compile the bulk of their data on prep players. Injuries, one scout said, were partly to blame.

"He goes from dominator to missing in action," said Van Coleman of *Future Stars*, a publication devoted to evaluating prep talent.

Said former UNLV assistant coach Mark Warkentien: "If you're fifteen or sixteen, you're tall and you do pretty good, we shower you with greatness. Everybody tells the kid how he's so good. He started reading all of his stuff in the newspaper and these scouting services and he doesn't work on his game. It retards progress."

Temkin recalls a football recruit out of Battle Creek, Michigan in 1992 named Reggie Vick, who some regarded as the best quarterback in the Midwest. Vick, scouts maintained, was being recruited by Michigan State, Vanderbilt, Iowa State, Nebraska and Wisconsin. The 5-10 Vick eventually signed with Eastern Michigan, a program which has won just seven games from 1990-92.

In 1990 the Colorado football team shared the national championship with Georgia Tech and was a contender for one in 1989, yet didn't make anyone's Top 10 recruiting rankings. The Buffaloes' 1987 recruiting class featured future NFL players Eric Bieniemy and Alfred Williams, but couldn't crack the Top 10. Colorado's only Top 10 recruiting class in the '80s was its first when *Blue Chip* magazine ranked the Buffaloes seventh. The bulk of those players were seniors in '83 and '84 when Colorado finished 4-7 and 1-10.

The highest rated class recruited by former UNLV men's basketball coach Jerry Tarkanian was in 1989 when George Ackles, David Butler and Moses Scurry were recruited from the junior college ranks. Neither of these players are currently playing in the NBA. "It was the highest rated class," says Warkentein, "but it wasn't the best. The most important things in recruiting is to get the pieces of the puzzle that fit rather than the biggest or prettiest piece of the puzzle. When you have pieces that don't interlock, it doesn't mean anything. A lot of times less is more. Sometimes we recruited subs to be seventh men who accepted that role and it was better than getting a great player who wouldn't accept it."

In football, schools such as Miami, Notre Dame and Michigan consistently snatch Top 10 recruiting classes. Over the last ten years, these schools have a combined winning percentage of .781, a good indication that the schools are evaluating and recruiting great athletes. This, however, is not proof that scouts are usually correct. Frank Beamer's football recruiting classes at Virginia Tech are seldom ranked among the nation's elite. But Beamer's a fundamentally sound coach, and the Hokies execute with undeviating precision. He has the adroitness of taking raw athletes and molding them into functional football players by their senior season. Following the 1997 football season, Beamer's 10-year record at Virginia Tech (61-51-2) is nothing fancy, but his 16-year career record is a hardy 103-74-4. It appears Beamer is doing his job well without trumpets blaring over his recruiting classes.

Most scouts remain hidden in the background and conduct business without involving themselves in the quirks of the recruiting process, yet some can be unethical. Tom Krug, a quarterback from Los Gatos, California who signed with Notre Dame in 1993, says he had a negative experience with a West Coast-based talent scout.

Krug was being recruited heavily by Notre Dame and USC, the scout's alma mater. The Fighting Irish were making a play for another quarterback, Ron Powlus of Berwick, Pennsylvania. Powlus, who was considered the best quarterback out of Pennsylvania since Miami Dolphins All-Pro Dan Marino, led Berwick to a 15-0 record and won a national championship by *USA Today*. He was named player of the year by 10 publications as a senior. The scout insisted that Notre Dame wasn't going to sign Krug to a National Letter of Intent because Powlus was headed to the school, and Krug should consider USC. Krug said he talked with the scout on five different occasions.

"From the beginning he was calling me and telling me to go to SC," Krug said. "He tried to set me and USC up all the time. In the beginning of the recruiting process I was like, 'Yeah, that sounds great.'"

"As I was leaning more and more toward Notre Dame, he started to come out with different excuses... (He'd say) things like, 'Did you hear Powlus is probably gonna go there? I heard they might not sign you because they had Powlus.'"

The scout angrily denies he attempted to steer Krug to his alma mater. "That's insane," he said. "As far as Tom Krug goes, I can't explain why he would say that since it was my personal opinion that (he) was a marginal Pac-10 candidate. Number one, it's ridiculous that I would want to do it because it's none of my business. My business is tracking athletes, not funneling athletes. I never in my life talked with Tom Krug five or six times. I talked with him probably twice."

Krug eventually signed with the Fighting Irish. He said he fell in love with the South Bend, Indiana, campus because nearly every building had a slice of history. He football career was later cut short because of a back injury.

If what Krug says is true, what the scout did is not against NCAA rules and the organization doesn't have the power to punish the scout. "Talent scouts spend a lot of time talking with these kids," Temkin says. "They become pals. To what extent do they become advisers? I don't know. Do they talk up their own schools?"

Recruiters have limited access to you, and they need to know more about the players. Most scouts are in business to provide information for coaches, players and fans, but college athletics is a bold multi-million dollar venture and your signature on a National Letter of Intent could mean the difference between a losing season and a national championship. Scouts do not have to follow NCAA rules in regards to gathering information on your comings and goings to colleges, and most earn money from college coaches who purchase their scouting services. What if a college coach approached a scout and told him he'd pay him a large sum of money if he were able to deliver a number of bona fide blue chippers in his direction? It's possible. These talent scouts have a lot to gain. Some will even go a step further.

Temkin recalls conducting research on a Chicago-based boys basketball talent scout who hovered around junior high and high school basketball programs. He'd pass out literature to the players for a summer traveling team. The attractive schedule included trips to Nebraska, Long Beach, California and Las Vegas. The scout was also recruiting players for summer league competition for high school and college players.

The coaches were concerned that the scout was a front for another high school and that he was recruiting players, and the Chicagoland area high school coaches have been known to start recruiting players in junior high. Temkin said the scout was setting up an ACT preparatory program and bragging about finding players summer jobs. The scout's name had been dropped enough that Temkin felt it was time to write a story.

"I had a phone number and I checked it out and it was registered to a business, Blankity Blank, Inc.," Temkin said. "So I sent away for the articles on the corporation. It said corporate purpose: 'To be agents.'"

A student-athlete who is involved with an agent at any time before his college eligibility is exhausted, is in jeopardy of having his eligibility stripped from the NCAA. Agents may contact you during your high-school years in an attempt to secure an advantage over other individuals who may wish to represent you once the player's collegiate eligibility has expired and are preparing for a professional athletic career. Many times, the agents will not represent actual agencies, but rather as individuals interested in your overall welfare and athletic career. The agent may shower you and your family with gifts or other benefits including money, clothing and cars. It is not worth the risk to get involved with these agents, especially when it could spoil your chance of earning a free and precious education.

# The Life of a College Recruiter

*Recruiting is like shaving. Do it every day or you will look like a bum.* —Anonymous

The primary recruiter may be the one who makes the most significant contribution to the success of an athletic program. One of the biggest misnomers in college athletics is that the head coach conducts the bulk of the recruiting. When you read in the newspapers that Joe Recruiter, the head coach at Big-Time University reeled in one of the best recruiting classes in the country, chances are Recruiter's assistant coach did the majority of the strenuous leg work. That's why when people hear of an assistant taking a head coaching position at a mid-level Division I school, the question may pop up, "Where did this coach come from?"

That person probably got the job because they worked diligently on the never-ending recruiting trail. They lured championship athletes and won plenty of games. You've heard of trickle-down economics? This is trickle-down success in college athletics. Besides, most recruiters strive to become head coaches so they won't have to be as involved in the recruiting process.

Highly regarded recruiters at national-level programs are organized and have the ability to evaluate talent. They are patient in dealing with whimsical teenagers and have a national awareness of talent. They are aggressive and obey the laws of their organization's governing body. The job of a recruiter is one of the most pressure-packed positions in all of college athletics.

The basketball recruiter's road work is highly intense. Nearly the entire month of July, the time of year for primary evaluations in basketball, an assistant coach may be on the road. Sure they may receive some vacation time, but at what cost when a yearning rival recruiter is lurking and waiting for the opportunity to make their pitch? During basketball games, these assistant coaches are sharply groomed, sometimes wearing the finest in tailored suits and dresses. They come off as people who do little work while the head coach works the sidelines. Yet the best recruiters are up until the wee hours of the morning attempting to round up the program's precious future. They write letters, plan road schedules, and spend hours on the phone trying to sell their programs.

They ask themselves many questions: *How can I sign Joe Athlete? How can I get an edge? How can I secure the program's future?* It's a tough job, because if recruiters fail to sign high-quality athletes, they may find themselves unemployed. That's why some college recruiters can be aggressive and at times shoddy, but these salesmen have to eat...or starve.

To better understand the life of a recruiter, let's take a look at one football recruiter and one men's basketball recruiter.

✳ ✳ ✳ ✳ ✳

Jeff Hawkins, former recruiting coordinator at Tulane University, had a sketch for reviving the football program. It called for raising the player's self-esteem both on and off the field. The coaching staff insisted that the players get involved in the New Orleans community and do charity work.

"A reporter asked me once if helping others is going to translate into wins and losses," Hawkins said. "When you help people, you feel good about yourself and these players haven't felt good about themselves in quite sometime."

When coach Buddy Teevens, Hawkins and the rest of the coaching staff arrived at Tulane in 1992, there were only 12 players able to bench press 300 pounds. "You look at Florida State, they have All-Americans sitting on the bench," Hawkins said. "We don't."

Hawkins was a talented, aggressive defensive tackle and end at Bridgewater State College in Bridgewater, Massachusetts an NCAA Division III school, from 1976-80. He used his small college background to his advantage in recruiting for Tulane. "I try to let kids know out there that there are other options," he said. "I'm in a business where I turn down a lot more kids than I recruit. This might sound funny coming from a recruiter in Division I football, but there are other things than football. That's the truth."

Hawkins, who holds a bachelor's degree in physical education, only deals in verity. If the father of a student-athlete calls him and tries to convince him that his son is a Division I prospect even though he's just 5-foot-8 and 185-pounds, Hawkins informed the father, ever so gently, that he wasn't the type of athlete Tulane University was seeking.

"Sometimes kids will call me up and say I'm 5-10, 185 pounds and I play offensive line," he says. "They say, 'No, I'm not a great size, but I've got a lotta heart and I know I can get it done.' Letting the air out of someone's bubble isn't a pleasant thing, but you have to make a positive out of it. You have to be honest about it."

Hawkins received his first Division I-AA opportunity when he accepted an assistant's position on Teevens staff at Dartmouth in 1987. He remained at Dartmouth for five seasons before joining Teevens at Tulane in 1992. Tulane was Hawkins first experience as a recruiting coordinator.

For his first seven months at the school, Hawkins took just one day off—Christmas. "I was thinking about recruiting on Christmas Day," he admits, "but I didn't come into the office." During the summer of '93, he was allowed five weeks vacation, but Hawkins, trying to lift a program which has participated in only one bowl game in it's history, took only 11 days off. Seven of those days were spent working at a football camp. "Maybe I don't think I'm as smart as everyone else," Hawkins said. "That's why I put so much into it."

Hawkins likens his role with that of a band leader. The assistant coaches who do the road work play the instruments. The type of sound the Tulane coaching staff plays is one of the keys to its recruiting success. The Green Wave's music has to be better than everyone else's. He has to make the sound so pure that the recruit doesn't want to hear another band's production. "I lay out all the positive things about Tulane, the football program and New Orleans," Hawkins said. "I think a kid is doing himself a disservice by not coming to Tulane."

The imperative ground work for Hawkins began the week following National Letter of Intent week in February when he combs through a list of over 3,000 prospects. He received a list of recruits from scouting services and mails prospects cards to high school coaches across the nation. He sifts through the feedback then gives the assistant coaches their geographical areas. Tulane rated its recruits from 1-5, with 5 being the highest rating.

"If they (one of the assistant coaches) come back and say, 'This kid can't play' well then that kid can't play," said Hawkins, who seldom overrules an assistant coach.

In April the coaches contact high schools for grades and see if the student-athlete qualified for admission. Video tapes of recruits played a major role in evaluations because of the NCAA's limitations on evaluations. Division I coaches have four evaluation periods during the recruiting calendar year from March 1 to May 31 of the following year. In May, coaches can make off-campus evaluations and the list is trimmed to about 1,000 a year. During June, July and August, coaches can't leave their campuses for evaluations. High school summer dismissal makes it rather difficult to obtain student-athletes' grades. In September and October, the list is down to about 400 names. Because the football season has started, coaches try to obtain senior footage of recruits. November is another evaluation period, but the coaches are still coaching their teams for the current season, and it is difficult to evaluate talent. Still, coaches attempt to see as many recruits as possible and the list is now about 200. By December and January, the list is prioritized and the staff figures out how many scholarships they have to offer.

Hawkins' responsibilities, and charm, turn up a notch during the meaningful official visits. "If they come to the dance," Hawkins says, "then they come to the prom." In 1993, Tulane had 53 official visits, tendered offers to 25 recruits and signed 18.

"If you ask a recruiter they normally say for every four kids they offer, one says yes," Hawkins said. "I'm not a mathematician, but 18 out of 25 is pretty good. The key is getting the kids on campus and I think that's true for most schools."

And once the athlete arrives on campus, then the real games begin.

✳ ✳ ✳ ✳ ✳

Tracy Dildy, an assistant men's basketball coach at the DePaul University, is unlike most coaches on the college level. He was an extremely talented student-athlete and was heavily recruited before he graduated from Dr. Martin Luther King High School in Chicago in 1985. He was a member of the first King High team coached by Landon "Sonny" Cox in 1982.

Cox first saw Dildy as an eighth grader at a YMCA on Chicago's South Side. Even at the precocious age of 14, Dildy understood the responsibilities of a point guard. "He was the best point guard I'd ever seen," Cox says. "I still haven't coached a better point guard than Tracy."

Cox was so taken by Dildy that he decided to try something that no other coach in the state of Illinois had ever done before when he tossed Dildy the keys to the King's offense and let him drive as a freshman. "Isiah didn't even do that," said Dildy, referring to Detroit Pistons guard Isiah Thomas, who prepped at St. Joseph's High School in suburban Westchester, Illinois.

A 6-foot point guard, and a player with adroit ball-handling skills and intelligence, Dildy was the first in a growing generation of Chicago area lead guards with a manner clearly influenced by the dauntless Thomas.

One night in a Chicago summer league game legend has it Dildy even sat the master down and taught him a thing or two. Dildy was just a few months removed from high school, while Thomas was already a budding NBA legend. Thomas had a reputation of punishing young lead guards if they styled too frequently. Dildy's team met Thomas's group in what was thought to be easy pickings for the veteran. Dildy, the story goes, went to work on Thomas like no other guard in Chicago summer league history. Dildy drove through the lane religiously and pilfered the ball from doubting Thomas so many times that Dildy was nearly led away in shackles. In the end, Dildy finished with 18 points, zillions of assists and steals before he called it a night. As he went to the bench and ran a towel over his sweaty face, Thomas beckoned, "C'mon back! C'mon back!" Thomas was embarrassed, angry. How could a teenager school me in front of all these people? Dildy just waved his hand back at Thomas. The game was over...check mate...so the story goes.

But even his talents couldn't prevent him from taking a strange recruiting ride.

During Dildy's first three years at King, he received letters from recruiters, a practice which is now allowed only for junior and senior student-athletes. By the time Dildy became a senior, the recruiting process became so hectic he moved out of his mother's apartment and across town with his brother Kevin. San Diego State, Iowa, Cincinnati,

Illinois, Wyoming, Southern California and Arizona State were the most persistent callers. "I was averaging around 12 calls a night," he said. "At first, you like the attention but during my senior year it got to be a bother."

Eventually Dildy, who handled most of his recruiting, established ground rules for recruiters to limit the seemingly endless calls. Of course, not all recruiters followed the agenda, and those schools were quickly eliminated. "There were coaches trying to track down my girlfriend's number and my friends' numbers," he said. Still, the level-headed Dildy managed to get stuck in some of the droppings of the recruiting world.

Dildy was so confused about which school he wanted to attend, he verbally committed to two schools—San Diego State and another school he refused to name. The other school's coach flew to Chicago to take Dildy out to dinner to celebrate, but when he arrived, he was stunned to read in a local newspaper that Dildy was headed to California.

"Both of the schools were great places and both of the coaches were great coaches," Dildy said. "It was one of those cases where I wish I could have been two people."

San Diego State, Dildy says, made a lasting impression early. The coaching staff called directory assistance in Chicago and asked for all the Dildys listed. They called every one, including some distant relatives, until they reached the correct Dildy.

He enjoyed two seasons at San Diego State, but after coach Smoky Gaines resigned, Dildy returned home to think about whether to remain at the school or transfer. During a Chicago summer-league game, Dildy bumped into Rick Pryor, an assistant coach at Illinois-Chicago and a close friend. Dildy and Pryor chatted and he decided to visit Illinois-Chicago. Dildy, a two-year starter at San Diego State, liked the environs at UIC and decided to play the remaining two seasons of his college eligibility with a program, and people, he was familiar with.

After Dildy finished his eligibility at UIC in 1990, he wanted to explore professional basketball opportunities and his agent set up tryouts with a few teams in the Continental Basketball Association. Dildy was eventually drafted by the CBA's Rockford Lightning, but while getting in shape for his tryout, he sprained ligaments in his ankle and was unable to attend the training camp. At the same time, Pryor accepted the head-coaching position at Chicago State University. Pryor's assistant job at UIC was available and Dildy decided to take a stab at coaching. Before the injury, Dildy, despite all of his maturity and leadership qualities, never thought about working the sidelines.

"A lot of people used to tell me, 'Man, you would be a great coach,'" he said. "They said, 'You should get into coaching.' I guess it was because of the position I played and the leadership ability I always had. I was capable of running a team, but I never really paid attention to it. I was a basketball *player.*"

Now at DePaul, Dildy's workhorse attitude carries over into recruiting. He says he can't compete with some of major universities, but he will outwork them. "They may send a kid a piece of mail once a week, I have to send that same kid mail five times a week," he said. "You have to bust your butt."

At the beginning of the recruiting season in July, Dildy will start with about 90 names on his master list filled with underclassmen, mostly juniors who will become seniors in the fall. He then mails questionnaires to the prospective student-athletes. "You'll be lucky to get back 45," he said.

He's allowed to send questionnaires and the school's summer-camp information to freshman and sophomores. Dildy sends juniors mail three times weekly and seniors nearly every day.

When the questionnaires are returned, Dildy tries to find out which camps, tournaments and summer-league games the players will attend. On July 1, recruiters can make telephone calls to student-athletes and for the following three weeks they can evaluate talent on the summer-camp circuit. The task of coordinating the college coach's summer schedule with the player's interested in the program is tedious. Dildy irons plenty of DePaul University T-shirts for himself so the recruits know which school he represents.

"You're out to see him, and you have to make sure he sees you," says Dildy, who primarily recruits in Chicago and the Midwest. "You have to let him know that you are really interested and you're just following up."

For three weeks Dildy will spend the majority of his time on the road, and staff at DePaul will hit at least 15 different cities during the recruiting period. Dildy will add more names, and delete several, but after the summer circuit, it's time for Dildy to make his first pitch to recruits.

The home visit is the time to make the initial play. Following the home visit, comes the official or campus visit where Dildy will invite recruits to take in the surroundings of DePaul. After the official visit, Dildy and the UIC staff will attempt to sign the recruit. In between the home visit and official visit, Dildy will mail hundreds of letters and will make half as many phone calls to recruits. But when the wooing process is over and the recruit's signature is on the National Letter of Intent, the celebration begins.

Such was the case when while at Illinois-Chicago, Dildy signed Sherell Ford in 1991. The 6-7 Ford was named the *Chicago Sun-Times* Player of the Year in 1990-91 after leading Proviso East High School in suburban Maywood, Illinois, to a 32-1 record and the Illinois Class AA state championship. University of Michigan forward Juwan Howard was runner-up to Ford for Player of the Year honors. Ford, who sat out his freshman season in 1991-92 because of Proposition 48, decided on UIC ahead of schools such as Illinois, UNLV, Michigan and Michigan State. "We could stick our chest out for that year," Dildy said. "But it's back to the drawing board after that."

Notes:

## Summer Camps

Reebok Summer Football Combines
Women's Basketball Coaches Association Camps
Nike All-American Camp

Summer camps have taken on a significant importance since college athletics became a booming industry in the last 20 years. In basketball, the days are nearly gone when you could have a solid senior season and earn an NCAA Division I scholarship. Because of the nation's numerous summer camps and tournaments, a student-athlete's senior year is almost rendered meaningless in terms of earning a scholarship.

I remember attending a basketball game as a youngster when Glenn "Doc" Rivers was a senior at Proviso East High School in Maywood, Illinois. On that chilly December evening, Proviso East, which was ranked No. 1 in the state, was playing rival Proviso West and the hoopla surrounding the game was at a feverish pitch. Then, like a modern-day rock star, in strolled Ray Meyer, who was at the time the coach at DePaul University, to watch Rivers. DePaul was the No. 1 team in the country, and nirvana swept the gymnasium. Proviso East vs. Proviso West with the proverbial Ray Meyer, who rarely traveled to watch recruits, taking in the festivities. You couldn't ask for anything more.

Those days have become melodious memories since 1982 when the NCAA introduced the early-signing period. The early-signing period, which allows recruits to sign in November instead of waiting until April, was designed to curb some of the pressure on recruits so they could concentrate on playing their senior year without the added burden of recruiters constantly calling. Also, the presumption was that the longer the recruiting process goes on, the more dirty deals could be executed. Rivers, one of the top rated players in the Class of 1980, was under immense pressure to sign with DePaul but eventually signed with Marquette University in Milwaukee.

Yes, winning a state championship during your senior year is something you will cherish forever, but there is a chance you will not accomplish the feat in front of a big-time college recruiter. Recruiters have an intense three-week block in July to evaluate student-athletes through the summer camps, and the ambiance of having a successful coach walking into a gym filled with fans to watch a high school student-athlete has faded.

The exposure camps for basketball have also been given a face lift over the past decade and its immediate future will be altered even more. In 1993, the NCAA stepped in to put a stop to invitation-only camps which seemed to assist in helping the rich programs become more vibrant. As a result, Division I men's and women's basketball coaching staff members may attend summer basketball camps that are certified by the NCAA, and the restriction is for events that occur during the Division I summer evaluation periods in July. To gain NCAA certification, camps must pledge in writing that the camp would be operated in accordance with NCAA rules.

The invitation-only camps were well-received. They were largely backed by major shoe companies such as Nike and prize campers were given free tuition, transportation, and room and board, not to mention a new pair of sneakers to show their friends back home.

In the summer of '97, basketball youngsters were offered oodles of opportunities to showcase their talents, including the Adidas/ABCD Camp in Teaneck, N.J., the Nike All-American Camp In Indianapolis, and the Adidas/Big Time in Las Vegas.

The ABCD Camp and Nike overlapped in July and for the fifth consecutive summer, Nike didn't have all of the best talent under one roof.

In football, your senior year is still valuable and if you enjoy a solid year, you can still earn a scholarship. But preseason combines sponsored by Reebok popped up in the summer of '93 and were very successful. More and more college recruiters seek data from these combines because it will save their universities time and money.

Let's take a closer look at these summer camps and tournaments. First we will look at the Reebok Preseason Summer Football Combines. Second, we will take a look at the Women's Basketball Coaches Association's camps for female student-athletes which started during the summer of 1992. Third, we will look into the Nike Camp, which is the stick by which all other camps are measured. Keep in mind these are not the only exposure camps, just three of the most publicized and fruitful.

## Reebok Summer Football Combines

Former Brown football player Terry Tracey and Reebok product manager Pete Worley had a brain storming session one evening. From it came the idea of a high school combine for football players. Naturally it was also a vehicle to market Reebok's new preseason footwear.

"We wanted to get inside the kids' heads," Tracey said. "We had the great marketing concept for shoes, we had the product and the great advertising. But we really wanted to connect ourselves with the culture of the sport."

Reebok wanted to correlate itself with the competitive athletes' mindset of training during the preseason. Tracy and Worley kicked the idea around with Bruce Webber of *Scholastic Coach Magazine*. Webber liked the plan and implemented more ideas. First the trio named a preseason high school All-America team with 100 prospects. "We wanted to be the first to announce the up-and-coming stars on a preseason basis," Tracey said. The information was published in Webber's magazine with the objective of gaining exposure for the high school football players. Reebok then mailed 27,000 invitations to the nation's high-school coaches. The invitations asked the coaches to select three senior-to-be players from their teams with the most potential to play college.

The first combines were held in Los Angeles, Napa, California, Dallas, Texas, Columbus, Ohio and Boston. In Florida, the nation's most recruited state for football, Reebok held 22 mini combines. Dwight Thomas, the high school coach of Dallas Cowboys All-Pro running back Emmett Smith, helped organize the Florida combines. Some of the Florida cities included Tallahassee, Jacksonville, Tampa, Miami and Orlando.

These one-day six-hour combines provided the athletes the opportunity to demonstrate their skills against a list of performance criteria. The results of the athlete's performance on the field and in the weightroom were recorded and made available to college recruiters. Recruiters could then size up talent from the various parts of the country and determine who needed a closer look. The list of drills included the 20-and 40-yard dashes, 185-pound bench press, the shuttle run, vertical leap, standing broad jump, and the four-corner run. The athlete's height, weight and wing span were also measured.

The combines also featured motivational talks from NFL players such as Smith, who wears Reeboks, and included teachers speaking on the necessities of gaining college eligibility, remaining eligible and earning degrees. Former Syracuse University and New England Patriots coach Dick MacPherson was a speaker in Boston, and Smith was video taped for the combines in Florida. The athletes and the coaches participated at no cost, and an average of 400 athletes took part in each of the sessions. The information was mailed to all NCAA Division I and II schools.

"It's a valuable scouting device for the coaches because they don't have to travel across the country to see talent," said Michael Payton, manager of marketing and communications for Reebok sports. "They can just look at how quick the kid runs the 40-yard-dash."

The combines are now conducted in 26 states, and are usually held in late spring. They are considered positive because athletes of all skill levels receive exposure to college recruiters. The drawbacks are, a high-school coach can only nominate three players from his team. What about that fourth, fifth or sixth prospect? Will he get passed over by his more heralded teammates?

"All we're trying to do is get the coaches and players into the mindset that Reebok is the preseason place to be," Tracey said. "We asked coaches to bring kids they felt had the most potential to get into college. Then we would do our job to make that happen."

Before the Reebok combines, some coaches were skating a fine line between conducting camps, and holding tryouts, which is an infraction of NCAA rules. Quarterback Brady Batten of Bakersfield, California said he attended a one day camp at UCLA in 1993. Batten said the camp was free camp and the school supplied T-shirts but felt the UCLA coaches, "just wanted to check you out."

"You don't really do much there," said Batten, who eventually signed a National Letter of Intent with the University of Arizona. "They say you're going to learn new drills and stuff but basically they just want to film you and get you on tape so they can look you over."

One drill timed how quick his release was. "They lined four or five of the quarterbacks up and they counted to three and said 'Release it now.' I guess he was watching the release, or that's what it looked like to me anyway. I went out of there learning absolutely nothing except for a little bit about how the colleges work. They basically want to see what they've got."

## Women's Basketball Coaches Association Camps

The rise of the lucrative summer-camp circuit in girls basketball coincides almost exactly to the explosion in popularity of the sport on the college level. The women's Final Four has been sold out at each venue since 1993. With that growth spurt came the added pressure of fielding competitive teams each game. It was time, pacesetters believed, to start uncovering potential college All-Americans earlier. In 1992, the WBCA joined the summer-camp business with camps at four different sites: Pomona, California; St. Louis, Missouri; Rochester, New York and Chattanooga, Tennessee. The camps were held at the same sites in '93, and the four areas were selected by the NCAA. The camps have since been scaled down to two sites: Jefferson City, Tennessee and St. Louis, Missouri.

The camps were formulated in response to the members' request for an evaluation camp which was cost effective, and an environment that would allow coaches to recruit in a non-threatening atmosphere. WBCA members (which includes school affiliated in the NCAA, NAIA, junior college and high school coaches) are asked to submit names for recommendation to the camps.

In addition to going through basketball drills, the campers are treated to educational seminars on strength, conditioning and nutrition. They also provide the opportunity for courses on how to take the SAT and ACT as well as tips on self esteem. Initially there was a $75 fee which covered room and board and tuition. The tuition fee has since been waived and the campers attend the camps at no cost.

"I think it took a year for the word to get out to legitimize the camps," said the WBCA's Maria Ahmann. "Our kids can be seen and be trained by some of the top high school coaches in the country."

Yet by making this an invitation-only event, the word "elitism" pops up.

Arthur Penny, girls basketball coach at Chicago's Whitney Young High School since 1986, says the elitist attitude of the WBCA will keep his talented youngsters away from its camps. Penny has sent over 40 players to college including E.C. Hill, a first-team *Parade* All-America selection in 1990 who signed with Northern Illinois University and is now playing in the American Basketball League. Penny maintains he coaches many talented student-athletes, which is why selecting just a few players from his team for a camp is an insult to his program. He prefers the team camp approach where all of his players can be watched and evaluated by college coaches. Penny endorses camps like The Blue Star Camps, which are held all over the country.

"The Blue Star camps are a way of getting all my kids into college and not just my All-American kids," he said. "I don't want the WBCA to think I'm a negative person about their camp but they are only inviting the blue chippers. I deal with fifteen girls who can play."

"A kid like E.C. Hill is automatically going to stand out and get a scholarship, but if I take some more of my kids to these camps a college recruiter may take a look at her and say, 'Hey, I could really use this kid.'"

# Nike All-American Camp

Before the concept of invitation-only camps, top college prospects, and scores of non-prospects, attended Howard Garfinkel's Five-Star Basketball Camp to gain national exposure. Michael Jordan spent a week at Garfinkel's camp during his high school days along with a parade of other NBA stars. The theory went if a player could perform at a considerable level at Five-Star, he probably could play on the Division I level. But in 1985, Nike decided it was time for the finest talent to have a camp to themselves, to view how they would stack against their peers. They named it the Nike/ABCD All-American Basketball Camp.

The ABCD in the camp's title stood for Academic Betterment and Career Development and the players had to take classes from 9 a.m. to noon. However, schoolwork was secondary to displaying the nation's top schoolboy talent.

At Nike's assembly, a student-athlete was given a round-trip ticket to the campus of Princeton University in New Jersey for a week. The camp included seminars on study skills and how to pass college entrance exams. Recruiters maintain they lose something when attempting to evaluate a player during the not-as-competitive regular season, but at Nike they enjoy the opportunity to watch a player at least three times daily. Recruiters can dissect everything—including the player's heart.

Among the NCAA's rules is one that allows college coaches to look-but-not-touch the players during the talent-laden camp. When the camp was held at cramped Princeton, players walking on and off the court were instructed to glance the other way so coaches couldn't make eye contact. When the affair was moved to the University of Indianapolis, the Indiana Pacers' preseason facility, the players sat on bleachers separated from the coaches by yellow police tape. When it was held in the shimmering Hoosier Dome in Indianapolis, the setting is so spread out that it didn't matter what the coaches did.

Take a roll call and you'll find all the big names in college basketball—Arizona's Lute Olson, Georgetown's John Thompson, Georgia Tech's Bobby Cremins and Syracuse's Jim Boeheim. In the stands high above—as if he were on a worldly throne away from the peons—sits Dean Smith of North Carolina. He waits for recruits to spot him. Others from less renowned Division I schools do a lot of well-timed standing, stretching and head nodding. Having the right position and body language is important for the mid-level Division I coaches attempting to build a strong reputation. At times it's better theater than the one which takes place on the floor. The only place with a greater coaching presence is the annual Final Four.

Over 100 current NBA players have attended the Nike Camp, including such talent as Chris Webber, Penny Hardaway and Allen Iverson. "We don't take credit for them being NBA players," says Dusty Kidd a spokesman for Nike. "We feel it has helped them. All of the number one or two players in their state came to the camp and found out they weren't the number one or two player in the camp."

Exposure camps like Nike are needed because the NCAA leaves open a only small window for evaluation. Generally, four evaluation periods take place per year. Coaches have wondered out loud if that is truly enough time to see if a student-athlete can fit into their sometimes detailed systems. "It's an opportunity for the kids to showcase their skills and earn a scholarship," Kidd said. "If you didn't have a system like this, coaches would have to fly all over the country and that would cost them a lot of money to do that."

Yet the high school coaching community is divided on Nike's activities. When a player such as Webber decides it's time to step into the next level, Nike has first crack to offer him a fat shoe contract. Nike's pitch could be: "Hey Chris, we were good to you when you were just a high school basketball star...we can be better to you now."

*Detroit Free Press* award-winning columnist Mitch Albom wrote in his book *Fab Five* about the University of Michigan's basketball team in the early 90s about how Nike executives warmly greeted Webber and his father, Mayce, during a trip to the company's headquarters in Portland, Oregon. Webber had recently announced he was leaving Michigan after his sophomore season to play in the NBA. Webber and his father were taken to the employees' store where all Nike merchandise from shoes to carry-on bags was on display, Albom wrote. An executive told the Webbers to pick out anything they wanted.

Nevertheless, there are some who insist that camps such as Nike are needed. "I think Nike wants to give something back to the game because they aren't making anything off of it," said Steve Smith, basketball coach at Oak Hill Academy in Mouth of Wilson, VA who has poured his nationally ranked team into Nike apparel since 1986.

But there have been players who have been successful on the college and professional levels without being active over the summer. Wake Forest All-American Tim Duncan didn't attend any summer basketball camps as a youngster and still ended up being the No. 1 pick the 1997 NBA draft.

Bob Hambric of Simeon High in Chicago has only allowed a handful of his players to attend camps such as Nike. One of Hambric's best player, Deon Thomas, didn't attend Nike and earned Mr. Basketball and All-American honors in 1989 before attending the University of Illinois. Hambric said the key to gaining exposure for his team is playing an attractive schedule during the regular season, including participating in several in-state tournaments. While it helps to play in a high-profile city like Chicago, Hambric said the scouts will come if the youngster has college-level ability.

"If you run a good program and you produce teams year in and year out, you're going to get plenty of exposure," he said. "Even if it isn't a well-known program, if the kid can play, the word of mouth is enough to get a kid a scholarship. (The camps) are nothing but meat markets. A lot of times, they use your kid as a measuring stick to see how the other kids can play. Those camps are used as a contact point. Somebody within the organization becomes familiar and develops a relationship with the child and then they try to sell their particular school to the child."

Smith, who insists he doesn't recruit players for his program, has been accused of attempting to coax players into attending Oak Hill while coaching at Nike. All the while he continues to produce national powerhouse teams at his tiny Baptist boarding school in Virginia. One of Oak Hill's first big-time players was Rod Strickland, now a point guard with the Washington Wizards.

In 1992, Smith, whose team owns an incredible 126-3 record from 1989-93, incurred the wrath of Paul Jones, the coach at Kinston High School in Kinston, North Carolina. Kinston captured the North Carolina state championship in '92 featuring All-American junior Jerry

Stackhouse in its lineup. But before his senior season, Stackhouse, regarded as the most gifted player to come out of North Carolina since Michael Jordan, transferred to Oak Hill. North Carolina high school officials estimated that the state would lose $100,000 during the state championship tournament because of Stackhouse's departure. An incensed Jones, whose team was favored to repeat as state champions *with* Stackhouse in the lineup, quickly pointed out that Smith coached Stackhouse's team at the Nike Camp in '92. It was Smith's argument that he got involved with Stackhouse only after hearing that the All-American swingman had talked with at least one other private school. Stackhouse signed with the University of North Carolina during the fall of '92 as is now in the lineup of the Detroit Pistons.

"We don't operate like that," Smith said. "A lot of people think we recruit but we just don't. I receive at least 150 calls from parents and players each year who are interested in our program. After they make contact with us, then I get back to them."

In the seven years Mark Warkentien was a scout and recruiting coordinator at UNLV, he helped recruit current NBA players Larry Johnson, Stacey Augmon, Greg Anthony and Armon Gilliam to the Runnin' Rebels' campus. None of them participated at the Nike Camp, and UNLV played in three Final Fours and won the national championship in 1990.

Then there was the fervent story of former Virginia high school phenom Allen Iverson, now of the Philadelphia 76ers, which kept the basketball world buzzing throughout the busy summer of 1993.

Iverson, regarded as the nation's top point guard, was sentenced in September 1993 to five years in prison for participating in a violent fight at a Hampton, Virginia bowling alley in February '93. Iverson spent four months in a minimum security prison in Virginia before Gov. L. Douglas Wilder granted conditional clemency to Iverson and ordered his release on furlough so he could continue his high school studies. Wilder ordered Iverson to get family counseling, observe a nightly curfew and not play sports while on furlough.

Before Iverson was put behind bars, Nike made a move that questioned how young, talented student-athletes are treated.

Just two hours after showcasing his impressive skills at the Nike Festival in July of that year, Nike official agreed to fly Iverson back on a Thursday to Virginia from Indianapolis where the camp was held, to appear in court for the bowling alley incident. When the trial ran longer than expected and broke for the weekend, Nike flew Iverson back to the camp for its all-star game that Saturday and then back for the conclusion of the trial. Nike's stance was that Iverson was innocent until proven guilty, and if they refused to include him in the Festival, it would have sent a poor message to America's youth. The trip, however, may have done Iverson more harm than good.

Before the verdict was handed down, Assistant Commonwealth's Attorney Colleen Killilea, who prosecuted Iverson, borrowed the company's advertising slogan in her closing argument. "Now," Killilea said facing Judge Nelson T. Overton, "it's our turn to just do it."

Nike wasn't finished in 1993.

The company said it was ashamed after they learned they might be responsible for eligibility problems for 37 of the nation's top high school basketball players. Players faced eligibility problems with their state high school athletic federation for accepting $100 gift certificates and practice gear worth nearly $300 while participating in an all-star camp in Beaverton, Oregon.

Nike held a two-day, four-game camp in September 1993 after the start of the school year to meet NCAA regulations. The shoe company failed to check with the National Federation and its 50 state associations to see if the camp violated its rules. Besides the gift certificate, Nike gave the players round-trip airline tickets along with shoes, practice jerseys, shorts, socks, T-shirts and sweatshirts.

Tennessee's top two high school basketball players nearly had to sit out the 1993-94 season for taking part in the Nike event. Ron Mercer of Goodpasture High School in Nashville and Lorenzen Wright of Booker T. Washington High in Memphis were sent letters from the Tennessee Secondary Schools Athletic Association informing them they were not eligible to play. Mercer was the state's Mr. Basketball following the 1992-93 season as a sophomore. They later had to serve a short suspension and were allowed to play.

The penalties handed down to Mercer and Wright were the most stringent of any of the players from the 19 states who took part in the event. In Illinois, senior Bryant Notree of Chicago Simeon and sophomore Ronnie Fields of Chicago were suspended for four games. In Mississippi, the state's High School Activities Association considered a one-game suspension against All-American Jerod Ward. The majority of the players simply had to return the gift certificates in order to restore their eligibility.

There are exposure camps other than Nike or Adidas that are held during the summer where college recruiters are present. The Nike Camp is a week-long event and college coaches have another two weeks to recruit after that camp is over. You should ask your high-school coaches about the different summer camps, or contact the NCAA for more information.

What does all of this mean to a player? The scouting services, the camps. Do they measure a player on the basis of how well they play against fellow prep players or do they measure college potential? Is the 60th rated player in the country, that much better than the 61st-rated player or not as good as the 10th, 20th, or 30th? Former Tulane basketball player Michael Christian knows exactly what they mean.

As a high-school phenom, Christian was a 6-foot-3 guard full of basketball liveliness, with a roaring vertical leap. He ran the point or shooting guard positions with flawless, veteran like ability. His jump shot was pure, without error. A native of Denver, Christian realized he was a Division I prospect early in his career. As a youngster, Christian honed his game by battling older players, and by the time he was an eighth grader, he knew he would attend a big-time university. Christian attended the Nike Camp as a sophomore during the summer and dazzled the scouts with his explosive quickness and uncanny shooting range. The following summer prior to his senior year, Christian was considered the No. 1 point-guard prospect in the nation by recruiting mavens. A few point guards rated a step below Christian in the Class of '86 included Rumeal Robinson, now a member of the Charlotte Hornets, and Greg Anthony, of the New York Knicks. But Christian suffered a severely broken leg after the third day at the Nike Camp in 1985, and missed his senior season at Mullen Prep. At the time, Christian was the third rated player at the camp behind Terry Mills, who went on to play at Michigan, and J.R. Reid, who earned All-America honors at North Carolina. Reid is a member of the Charlotte Hornets and Mills is currently playing for the Detroit Pistons.

Despite the injury, recruiters buzzed around Christian because of his unlimited star potential. One scouting service felt so moved by Christian's aptness, they came to the disputable conclusion he was, "Jerry West with a jump shot."

"Everyone else was reading the same articles I was, so as a result, I had to be prepared every time I went out on the court," said Christian, who signed with Georgia Tech in November 1985. "As a young person, (the attention) feels good, and you're going to get a chip on your shoulder a little bit. It's stupid to say you're not. To be admired like that and be a young man at the age of 15, 16 or 17 and have the whole country look up to you, you have to have some kind of ego about it."

And with great players come great recruiting tales that almost transform into folklore. There was one account which Christian says was highly amplified by ESPN basketball analyst Dick Vitale about Christian's official visit to the University of Illinois. Christian, the story goes, was surrounded by Illinois alumni and players, being patted on the back and told what a great player he was. He was Michael Christian, the nation's third best player and one of Illinois top recruits. Meanwhile, Kendall Gill, a willowy soft-spoken youngster from Matteson,

Illinois was standing off to the side drowning in the Christian circus. Gill eventually signed with Illinois and led the Fighting Illini to the Final Four in 1989. Gill plays for the New Jersey Nets, and is one of the rising young stars of the NBA.

The story irks Christian.

"That's Vitale pumping that crap up," he said. "Kendall is a good player as you can see. He was a good player then. I was just a little more outgoing than he was and I'm used to being around a lot of people."

After signing with Tech, Christian also sat out the 1986-87 season after re-breaking the leg in a pick-up game. He played just seven games for Tech and left the school before, "things got out of hand." Christian didn't burn any bridges with coach Bobby Cremins and his staff, which at the time included assistant coach Perry Clark, the man who recruited Christian out of high school. After leaving Tech, Christian took a long look into the future. He had been thinking about the NBA since he was a junior in high school and after the big splash he made at Nike. Would it be so bad if he *didn't* turn out to be an NBA superstar? Would it matter if he didn't become the next Jerry West?

"I learned a lot and it made me grow up," he said. "I knew that I couldn't take things for granted. The main thing was I didn't close any doors (at Georgia Tech)."

Christian resurfaced at Delgado Community Junior College in New Orleans where he was the nation's seventh leading scorer during the 1988-89 season with a 27.0 points per game average. At the same time Tulane decided to field a basketball team again after the program was discontinued following a point-shaving scandal during the 1984-85 season. The rebirth of the Tulane program was entrusted to Clark, who earned the reputation as one of the top recruiters in the game while at Georgia Tech. During his tenure at Tech, Clark signed Mark Price, John Salley, Duane Ferrell and Tom Hammonds, who are all enjoying productive careers in the NBA.

One of Clark's first recruits at Tulane was Christian. The first season, Christian and his Green Wave teammate endured through a painful 4-24 season in 1989-90. A picture was shown in the New Orleans *Times-Picayune* of Clark sitting on the bench and holding his head in hands, disheartened after yet another setback. Tulane bounced back in Christian's final season with a 15-13 record, and his scoring ability helped elevate the Green Wave off the ground and on the college basketball map.

Under Clark, Tulane is sleek and reborn and is growing into one of the powerhouses of college basketball. During the 1991-92 season, the Green Wave program flourished. Tulane finished 22-9, won the Metro Conference championship, and earned an NCAA tournament bid for the first time in school history. The Green Wave earned another NCAA bid during the 1992-93 season, and a National Invitational Tournament in 1993-94. Clark now signs big-name prospects such as Jerald Honeycutt, a 6-foot-9 two-time *Parade* All-American from Grambling, Louisiana.

Christian says he hasn't lost a step driving to the hoop, but he can't jump as high. Sounding like a grizzly veteran, he says he now has to outthink opponents. "It's still in my grasp," said Christian about playing in the NBA. "I just have to be in the right place at the right time."

There are several business opportunities for Christian established by his contacts in Atlanta and New Orleans. Christian now lives in Detroit and lists several contacts in the Motor City as well. He's weighing all of his options says Christian, who earned a degree in sociology in 1993.

He was considered one of the greatest players in the history of the city of Denver. The scouts elevated him into the pantheon of sainted guards of the past and he was rated one of the nation's top players after three days at a basketball camp. What does it mean to Michael Christian?

Nothing.

# Chapter 11

## Recruiting Stories

It seems as if each season presents at least one strange tale in the recruiting underworld. In 1993, nowhere was the seamy recruiting process better reflected than in Cincinnati and the recruitment of high-school basketball phenom Damon Flint. The story had all elements of a bad late-night B flick—unfounded accusations, NCAA rule violations, alleged division in the family, and a lawyer. All over a youngster whose jump shot is like the serenity of snowfall in winter.

The University of Cincinnati and Ohio State University, two teams who will become bitter rivals whenever they decide to play one another, each badly wanted the 6-foot-5 swingman who had been highly regarded since his sophomore season at Woodward High School. Flint signed with Ohio State during the early signing period in November 1992, but he will never play for the Buckeyes because of alleged NCAA rule violations by members of the Ohio State coaching staff and Flint's high school coach, Jim Leon. Flint later signed with Cincinnati in May 1993 at the Cincinnati office of his lawyer.

It remains unclear how the events unfolded, but the NCAA declared Flint ineligible to play at Ohio State because of coach Randy Ayers' admission that he and former Buckeye assistant, Paul Brazeau, who left to coach at the University of Hartford before the 1992-93 season, gave money to Leon to pay for a meal. Leon said Brazeau gave four nylon training bags to Flint and his teammates. In all, the NCAA found that Ohio State committed 17 rule violations, six of which stemmed from an October 30, 1991 meeting between Flint, then a high school junior, and Ohio State coaches.

Flint, Leon and three of Flint's Woodward teammates visited an Ohio State practice that day. Leon said that he and Ayers agreed to have dinner later with the young players. Oddly, Ayers suggested a sports bar called Damon's located less than a mile from the Ohio State campus. NCAA rules state that universities may not pay for recruiting visits for high school juniors nor arrange to meet them off campus. Leon said he was assured by Ayers and Brazeau that Damon's was on the Ohio State campus. After dinner, Leon said, Ayers, Flint and his teammates started to leave the bar when Brazeau pulled out three $20 bills and handed them to Leon to cover the bill. Once outside the bar, Leon said Brazeau got four bags from his car, and put them in the trunk of the car in which Flint was riding.

The NCAA said Brazeau bought a fast-food meal for Flint and Leon while visiting Woodward on December 9, 1991, and that Ayers later had a quick face-to-face meeting with Flint. Ayers also offered his condolences over the death of Damon's mother, Donna Walker, and had a meeting with his grandmother, Katherine Allen, at a practice at Woodward before Ohio State's NCAA tournament game in Cincinnati in March 1992. Yes, offering condolences to a grieving youngster, who happens to be one of the top junior basketball players in the country, is an NCAA violation. To this day, no one knows who dropped the dime.

Leon was accused by Flint's uncle Bryan Allen of knowingly taking Flint on the Ohio State trip and others without the consent of the family in an effort to get Flint ruled ineligible to attend Ohio State. Allen's theory is that Leon wanted Flint to attend Cincinnati, while Allen freely admits he wanted his nephew to attend Ohio State.

"I just wanted him to get away from home so he'd have the opportunity to mature," Allen said.

Allen maintains that Leon would always call and tell Katherine, his grandmother and legal guardian, where he was taking Damon when they visited college campuses to "play basketball." He informed the Allens of every outing except the trip to Ohio State that caused Flint to lose his eligibility.

"He (Leon) would call and say, 'Me and Damon are going to the U of L (Louisville) to play basketball,' or (We're going to) 'UK (Kentucky) to play basketball,'" Allen said. "Why didn't he call when they went to Ohio State? That, I don't understand."

Before the violations were announced to the public, Leon called Katherine to inform her of the infractions, and Katherine relayed the violations back to Bryan. Allen said Leon left Katherine with a puzzling message that sent her seething in anger.

"He said 'Don't worry, Miss Allen, I can get Damon into UC.'" Allen said. "My mother was really angry when he said that. My mother knew something was up. I think he was coaxing Damon into going to UC, that's where he wanted him to go all along."

Several days after Flint's eligibility was stripped, Allen said Leon called Katherine and told her he was taking Flint to play basketball. The family later discovered Leon set up a meeting between Flint and Cincinnati head coach Bob Huggins.

"My sister (Sharon) got wind off it," Allen said. "She called Bob Huggins and asked him, and he told her, 'Yeah, I was supposed to meet with Damon today at 6:30.' My mother was highly upset."

The next time Katherine saw Leon in public, Allen said she slapped him in the face. "Could you ask Leon about that hand print that's *still* on his face?" Allen said. Leon officially stepped away from the recruitment of Damon Flint.

"I didn't want that son of a bishop to have anything to do with Damon," Katherine said.

Leon denies all of Allen's accusations. He says the only thing he did wrong was taking the money from Brazeau for the off-campus meal. Leon says Flint looked up to his uncle and a lot of promises of spending time with Damon were left unfulfilled.

"Many times Damon said to me, 'Bryan's a big phony,'" Leon said. "I never asked Bryan for anything because Damon told me not to. He said the only person who needs to know anything was his grandmother. I love Damon, our relationship is very strong. That's all I care about."

Leon and many followers of Cincinnati prep basketball paint Allen as a washed up playground legend trying to relive his glory days through his talented nephew. Leon says Allen would hang around the Woodward practices, hoping to hook on as an assistant coach. He believes Allen wanted a slice of Flint's "potential earnings."

"I believe Bryan was on the take from Ohio State," Leon said. "A lot of people assumed I wanted him to go to Cincinnati. If that was the case, why would I let him (Flint) sign with Ohio State?"

After all, some say, Allen wanted Flint to attend a school away from Cincinnati, and Ohio State is more than two hours from Flint's home. Rumors surfaced that during Flint's official recruiting trip to Ohio State, Allen went along with Damon to eat dinner at Ayers' home. Also, rumors said there was money in one of the bags given to Flint from Brazeau, a payment to Allen in hopes of later providing Flint's signature on a National Letter of Intent.

"How much did I get?" Allen asked facetiously.

Several thousand dollars.

"Several thousand?" he replied, laughing. "That's a nice down payment on a house or a car, right? It's not true at all. I never got any money from Ohio State. I didn't eat dinner at Ayers' house. I just have Damon's best interest at heart."

Neither Allen nor Leon is close to Cincinnati attorney Lou Rubenstein, a long-time friend of Katherine, who was brought in to handle Flint's recruiting following the Ohio State ruling by the NCAA. Rubenstein maintains that after the infractions, Flint had only two choices—either attend Cincinnati, or fight the NCAA and become a Buckeye.

"Certainly Damon has done nothing wrong here," Rubenstein said. "We wanted to make sure he was well insulated from any claims that he had done anything wrong."

Rubenstein orchestrated Flint's release from the Ohio State Letter of Intent, and an acknowledgment from the NCAA's national letter committee. Nevertheless, Rubenstein wasn't accustomed to receiving feelers from aggressive college coaches, all of whom thought they had a shot at signing Flint. The feeding frenzy was on, even though Flint refused to take any more official visits.

Rubenstein did not return any calls from college recruiters unless Flint said it was okay. Over a two-week period, Rubenstein fielded over 50 calls from college recruiters. The media were just as unyielding. One radio station called Rubenstein at his home at 12:30 a.m. and asked if he represented Flint. "Yes," he replied. They wanted to ask him some questions. "I have just one question for you," Rubenstein recalls asking the uncompromising radio station. "Do you have a watch? Call me Monday morning in my office."

Click.

Several people were crammed into Rubenstein's tiny office as Flint prepared to announce where he would continue his education. "There were enough members of the media there that the temperature in the room went up 20 degrees from all the light," Rubenstein said. "It was hot as hell." Two reporters traveled from Columbus, where Ohio State is located, to attend the press conference. A reporter from *USA Today* was also present. One radio station asked Rubenstein if they could broadcast the event. *Live.*

With the stroke of a pen, Flint made Bob Huggins a happy man by signing with the University of Cincinnati.

But is Damon Flint happy? At worst, all anyone had accused him of doing was hanging around people who broke NCAA rules. For that, Flint could not attend the school of his choice and now has a different outlook on the world of college athletics.

"It's a whole different story now," Flint told Branson Wright of *The Lima* (Ohio) *News* "It's not like high school anymore where you play ball and have fun. College basketball is a business. You have to watch yourself. The hardest part was just waiting for everything to end. I'm sorry I'm not going to Ohio State but sometimes things happen for a reason."

During the 1993-94 season, Flint, a natural second guard was the starting point guard for Cincinnati, and led the Bearcats to the Great Midwest tournament championship. Meanwhile, inconsistent Ohio State finished 6-12 in the Big Ten and 13-16 overall. The main reason why the Buckeyes suffered through a losing season? The lack of a true point guard.

✳ ✳ ✳ ✳ ✳

Grover Kirkland, boys basketball coach at Northwestern High School in Flint, Michigan, went through a devastating recruiting onslaught with former player Glen Rice, a 1985 Northwestern graduate. It was so hectic that Kirkland, a talker of some renown, refuses to discuss the matter.

"There was never a game when there weren't two, three or four major college programs represented," said Phil Pierson of the *Flint Journal* who was the newspaper's high school beat writer at the time. "If the school wasn't represented by the head coach, then one of the top assistants was there."

The most frequent visitors who filed through Flint to see Rice included Iowa State coach Johnny Orr, Michigan State's Jud Heathcote and DePaul's Joey Meyer. Pierson recalls one night during the recruitment of Rice when Northwestern took on cross-town rival Flint Central and its two-sport All-American Terence Greene, who was also being recruited as a tight end by nearly all the Big Ten schools. Over 40 college coaches were in attendance.

Oddly enough, Rice signed with Michigan, a football power, while Greene brushed aside the football overtures and attended DePaul.

Also in Flint, Pierson recalls a strange tale regarding football stars Booker Moore and Rodney Feaster. Initially, Moore and Feaster wanted to attend college together, which sounded like a good idea to the fans in Flint. The problem was they kept hearing how great the plan was a little too often.

The evening before signing a National Letter of Intent, Moore decided to attend Penn State University, while Feaster wanted to remain close to home and sign with Michigan. To relieve the potential blitzkrieg of "Are you guys nuts?" and "I thought you were going to school *together!*" Moore and Feaster were hidden by their high school coaches in a local motel the night before they were to sign. They didn't want to be talked out of their decisions.

"I think only three people in Flint knew where they were," Pierson said.

✳ ✳ ✳ ✳ ✳

In 1993, 6-11 center Avondre Jones from Artesia High School in Lakewood, California received 50 letters per day from Southern California coach George Raveling in the two weeks leading up to Jones' announcement of where he would attend college. Jones' mother Vivian Ruffin and her husband also received 20 letters apiece each day from Raveling. Jones' teammate at Artesia, Charles O'Bannon, wanted Jones to attend UCLA with him, but Jones joined Raveling at USC. Jones made his announcement at a news conference in Lakewood, while O'Bannon's decision was shown live on a Long Beach cable television channel and broadcast live on an all-sports radio station in San Diego. Currently, Avondre Jones plays for Fresno State.

✳ ✳ ✳ ✳ ✳

Former UNLV men's basketball scout and recruiting coordinator Mark Warkentien, who was once the guardian of New York playground legend and San Antonio Spurs guard Lloyd Daniels, says he came across something peculiar while recruiting at a junior college one weekend in Moberly, Missouri.

Warkentien heard a player he was recruiting had decided to attend another school. Warkentien knew he couldn't trust second-hand information, so he asked a more reliable source, a rival recruiter, "Is he going to your place? Am I wasting my time?" The coach indicated Warkentien was still in the running along with the University of Missouri, but he was willing to discredit Missouri in favor of UNLV.

"He told me, 'If we can't get him, I'll help you with the kid,'" Warkentien said. "'I'll blow up Missouri.' He said, 'You have to make me a deal. You have to leave the kid alone.'"

"Leave the kid alone?" Warkentien thought, knowing the coach would probably damage the reputation of Missouri *and* UNLV if given the opportunity. You can't give a rival recruiter the edge.

So later that evening Warkentien invited the recruit to his hotel room to talk and catch a little ESPN for a few hours. When the recruit left it was late. Almost immediately after he departed the telephone rang. It was the recruiter he talked to earlier. "There must be honor among thieves!" the recruited bellowed. Warkentien was busted. But how? Was there a bug planted in the room? Not exactly.

Warkentien alleges that the staff at the Moberly hotel where he was staying was on the payroll of the college coach who told Warkentien to keep away from the recruit. Warkentien says the coach monitors comings and goings of rival coaches including how long they stay in the hotel and long-distance telephone calls. It's college recruiting...FBI style.

The following year, the recruiting evils hit Warkentien again.

Five major universities, including UNLV, were making a play for a high school All-American who had indicated he wanted to sign with the Runnin' Rebels. There was a catch, however, because one of the player's parents wanted cash in exchange for the player's signature on a National Letter of Intent. Warkentien, well aware that the NCAA was monitoring every UNLV move, told them, "No thank you."

The following week, the student-athlete signed with School A, but the school didn't announce it. Schools B, C and D then offered him some illegal inducements and the recruit said "no" to each. Warkentien thought it was peculiar that School A hadn't announced the signing of this recruit for several days. After all, he was a big-time player, one who could help any team to a national championship. UNLV would have certainly announced it. They would have sent faxes to every major newspaper in the country! But this isn't the real world. This is the world of college recruiting. Something is up, Warkentien thought. UNLV head coach Jerry Tarkanian told Warkentien to continue to pitch UNLV to the recruit. But first, Warkentien called someone close to the situation and was told, "Whatever you do, don't come back in."

The parents of the recruit tape recorded all the illegal inducements made by Schools B, C, and D; so when it was announced that he signed with School A, no one would attack the school. Of course, School A came through with its illegal offer.

Warkentien is now a scout with the Portland Trailblazers and has no interest in returning to college coaching, especially to the muddled world of recruiting.

Notes:

## Proposition 48

The roots of Proposition 48 began in 1982 when two separate groups who were concerned with the academic progress of college student-athletes met to come up with a basic plan. At the time college graduation rates were sagging and a former basketball star named Kevin Ross admitted he passed through Creighton University without a degree and without the ability to read.

The first group met in Sapelo Island, Georgia in the spring of 1982 to come up with a replacement for the rule known as the 2.000 Rule. The rule, which was enforced from 1971 to 1986, stipulated that every high school student-athlete was eligible to receive an athletic scholarship if they maintained a 2.0 grade-point average.

The Sapelo Island group drafted a proposal called Proposition 48, that required incoming student-athletes to achieve at least a 2.0 GPA in a college-prep curriculum and a 700 on the SAT's before they could receive an athletic scholarship. In September 1982, the Sapelo Island group gave its proposal to the American Council on Education (ACE), a trade association of the nation's leading universities. The American Council on Education had just established a committee for reform as well.

At the 1983 NCAA Convention, the ACE Committee submitted several proposals and the Sapelo Island proposal was among them. Well aware that SAT scores and college-prep requirements would hinder recruiting greatly, the athletic directors and faculty athletic representatives fought ACE's proposal. Eventually, Proposition 48 passed, but with compromise.

An amendment enabled high school student-athletes who didn't score high enough on the SAT or ACT to still receive an athletic scholarship. The "partial qualifier" as the student-athletes were called, had to sit out his freshman year. The proposal was bitterly opposed by most delegates from predominantly black schools who argued that the measure is racially and culturally discriminatory.

At the 1989 NCAA Convention, the Southeastern Conference proposed Proposition 42. This measure would have eliminated any student-athlete from receiving an athletic scholarship if they didn't score high enough on the SAT. Black college presidents were furious over Proposition 42. They felt the majority of African-American student-athletes would be precluded from attending college because they couldn't afford to go without an athletic scholarship.

Initially, Proposition 42 was voted down but within hours the measure was reintroduced and passed. Just days after Proposition 42 was passed, Georgetown men's basketball coach John Thompson announced he would boycott until the NCAA changed its stance on the proposal. A week after Thompson's boycott began, Proposition 42 was retooled. However, Thompson's walkout was a mere brush fire compared to the near explosion that happened at the 1994 NCAA Convention.

Two years earlier at the 1992 Convention, the reform-minded NCAA Presidents Commission reworked the rudiments of Proposition 48 once again and came up with Proposition 16. The new rule raised the number of core courses to 13 and hiked the minimum grade-point average in the core to 2.5. There was also a sliding index where a higher grade-point average in the core would offset a lower test score. The NCAA voted to enforce Proposition 16 by 1995.

Studies showed if Proposition 16 had been in place in 1988, nearly four of every 10 freshman football and basketball student-athletes would have been disqualified. The study was conducted by the academic research department of the NCAA. Of course, the study didn't take into account the main argument of Proposition 48 supporters that high school student-athletes will bring up their grades when challenged.

Two years later, just days before the 1994 Convention, the NCAA Council announced it would support a resolution that directed a complete and thorough review of Proposition 16. Members of the Black Coaches Association were the driving forces behind this evaluation. The BCA maintained, among other things, that literature on Proposition 16 wasn't getting out to high school student-athletes. The NCAA said they were also going to review a proposed scholarship reduction in men's basketball from 14 a year to 13.

A few days into the Convention, at the risk of drawing the wrath of the BCA, the Presidents Commission refused to budge on the issue of adding a scholarship for men's basketball. The basketball-scholarship issue overshadowed the overwhelming passage of the measure to delay and study Proposition 16 (311-10-2). Members of the BCA threatened to boycott the nation's college basketball games because of the NCAA's ruling on the scholarships. The planned boycott, which came to be known as "Black Saturday" fell on January, 15 1994—the birthday of the late Dr. Martin Luther King, Jr.

A day before the planned boycott, the BCA and the Congressional Black Caucus announced that the coaches had delayed the boycott because a branch of the Justice Department had offered to mediate the BCA's differences with the NCAA. During the 1994 Final Four in Charlotte, the BCA and the NCAA reached an agreement to avert a boycott. The agreement called for a study of the impact of the reduction in scholarships on educational opportunities for minorities. The agreement also called for an accounting of the needs of minorities when athletic reforms are considered, greater participation by female minorities and the restoration of a fourth year of athletic eligibility for student-athletes who are partial or non-qualifiers of Prop. 16.

In March 1994, the SAT, which first appeared in 1926, got its first major overhaul in two decades. The test allowed students to use calculators and better test critical thinking skills. Yet detractors maintained the revisions didn't address what they considered an underlying bias against women and minorities.

Cinthia Schuman, the head of the National Center for Fair and Open Testing, told *The Associated Press* in February of '94 that: "It's an attempt to make the SAT look like it will measure higher-order thinking skills. You really can't measure higher-order thinking skills in questions answered in one minute or less, or when students can't show their work or do anything except choose from preselected possibilities."

The Princeton-based Educational Testing Service, which administers the test, eliminated some of the passages in the verbal section but the passages were longer. The exam also included a pair of passages on the same subject, and the student had to compare. The revised SAT didn't contain a section on antonyms, and the test had more partial sentences which students had to complete.

The students were also allowed to use calculators for the mathematics section. The new version had 10 math questions without multiple-choice answers which students were required to calculate.

✶ ✶ ✶ ✶ ✶

In NCAA Division I, the minimum required SAT or ACT score must be achieved no later than the July 1 immediately preceding the student-athlete's first full-time college enrollment or by the end of the student-athlete's final term of secondary education. In Division II, the minimum required SAT or ACT score must be achieved before the student-athlete's first full-time college enrollment. In both divisions, the test scores must be achieved under national testing conditions on a national testing date. Please check with the SAT and ACT organizations for proper test dates.

# Test-Score Interpretations (Source: NCAA)

**1.** All prospective student-athletes, including natives of foreign countries, must achieve the minimum test score on a national testing date.

**2.** The following interpretations apply to the combination of test scores from more than one national testing date:

a. For student-athletes using the SAT, the highest scores achieved on the verbal and math sections of the SAT from two different national testing dates may be combined in determining whether the student-athlete has met the minimum test-score requirement.

b. For student-athletes using the ACT, the highest scores achieved on the student-athlete's subtests of the ACT from more than one national testing date may be combined in determining whether the student-athlete's composite score has met the minimum test-score requirement. Subscores from the version of the ACT in use before October 28, 1989, may not be combined with subscores from the enhanced version of the ACT introduced October 28, 1989.

c. Student-athletes whose combined composite test score from more than one ACT results in a fraction may round up a minimum of .5 to the next whole number. For example, 17.5 is changed to 18.0, but 15.2 is counted as 15.0.

**3.** The following criteria and procedures have been approved in regard to the SAT and ACT test-score requirement of Proposition 48 as it relates to learning-disabled and handicapped student-athletes who are in need of nonstandard testing:

a. The student-athlete must register for the nonstandard testing in the manner outlined by the testing services, which requires that the handicap or learning disability be diagnosed professionally and properly documented and confirmed.

b. The testing procedures followed must be those outlined by the testing service, and the people administering the test may not be a member of the high school's athletics department or an NCAA member school's athletic department.

c. The following documentation must be forwarded to the NCAA national office:

■ A copy of all documentation forwarded to the testing service for purposes of registering for the test, including the professional diagnosis of the learning disability or handicap.

■ The student-athlete's complete record of SAT or ACT scores.

■ A statement from the people administering the test that they are not a member of the athletics department at a high school or an NCAA member school.

d. A student-athlete who takes a nonstandard ACT or SAT must still achieve the minimum required test score. The test does not have to be administered on a national testing date. For Division I schools, the test must be taken by July 1 immediately preceding the student-athlete's initial college enrollment or by the end of the student-athlete's final term of secondary education. In some limited cases, exceptions to these requirements may be approved by the NCAA Council Subcommittee on Initial-Eligibility Waiver.

e. After the appropriate documentation has been received, the NCAA Academic Requirements Committee may then approve the student-athlete's completion of the test-score requirement on a case-by-case basis.

## Waiver of Proposition 48 Requirements (Source: NCAA)

The NCAA Council Subcommittee on Initial-Eligibility Waivers may grant waivers of the initial-eligibility requirements of this legislation based on objective evidence that demonstrates circumstances in which a student-athlete's overall academic record warrants the waiver of the normal application of this regulation. All appeals under this regulation must be initiated through a member institution that officially has accepted the student-athlete for enrollment as a regular student. Student-athletes should contact the schools he is interested in for more information regarding the NCAA's waiver process.

An exception may also be granted for a student-athlete who left high school after completion of his junior or senior year to enter a Division I or II school under an early admissions program on the basis of outstanding academic performance and promise. An exempted student-athlete must have maintained a 3.5 grade-point average on a 4-point scale and must have ranked in the top 20 percent of their class for the last four semesters completed in high school. All requirements of a qualifier (core curriculum and test scores) must be met except graduation from high school.

## Other Information Regarding Proposition 48 (Source: NCAA)

**1.** Requirements currently do not apply to Division III schools.

**2.** In order to implement Proposition 48, high-school officials are encouraged to complete a form (48-H) listing the core courses (as defined by the NCAA) offered at their high school. Copies of Form 48-H are available through the schools the student-athletes are interested in and the NCAA national office.

**3.** The General Education Development (GED) test may be utilized under certain specified conditions to satisfy the graduation require-ment of Proposition 48 but not the core-curriculum or test-score requirements. For more information, contact the NCAA.

A few years before Proposition 48 was implemented, former high school basketball All-American Chris Washburn was admitted to North Carolina State University with an SAT test score of 470. Former Tulane basketball star John "Hot Rod" Williams, who ended his college career with 1,841 points, was admitted to the university with a 470 SAT. The median score for regular students at Tulane was 1121 when Williams enrolled in 1981. Under Proposition 48, Washburn and Williams would have been ineligible to play as freshmen.

"It helps the freshman athlete get accustomed to college life," says one former coach. "I feel all freshmen should sit out their first year because it will help them academically. They'll spend one year hitting the books."

Yet many claim Proposition 48 has racial overtones against the African-American student-athlete. The NCAA's report showed graduation rates went up in 1986, but at the same time, there were also about 600 fewer African-Americans enrolled in Division I schools than in the three previous years. Critics are also uncomfortable with the fact that student-athletes must pay for his first year of school. Former Temple University basketball stars Eddie Jones and Aaron McKie were unable to score high enough on the SAT to become eligible as freshman, and each incurred nearly $12,000 in debt to pay for his first year. Jones and McKie are both high NBA first-round selection and will earn more than enough money to pay for their loans. However as high school seniors, both were considered long shots to advance to the next level.

"I think Prop. 48 is a bunch of mess," said Norwaine Reed, boys basketball coach at Buena Vista High School in Saginaw, Michigan. "These presidents and the media are in cahoots to eliminate black involvement in athletics. Proposition 48 is really another name for exclusion."

In a society based largely on the labeling of people, Reed makes a valid point.

Former Notre Dame student-athletes Tony Rice, who is African-American and John Foley, who is white, told *Newsday's* G.D. Clay that the stigma of Proposition 48 stayed with them before and after they entered the South Bend, Indiana institution.

Rice was a freshman at a Fighting Irish football pep rally in 1986 when a fan Rice met earlier turned to his child and said, "Hey that's Tony Rice. He's the dumb one."

In February 1993, Foley was interviewing for a position with a pharmaceutical company in Texas.

"Everything was going well in the interviews until about the third or fourth one," Foley told Clay. "Everything went well in the first two interviews; I thought I would get the job. I had to write an autobiography, and I said I had a tough time in high school. Then, I told them I was a Prop. 48 kid. As soon as I told them that, they dropped me off the list. It was like boom: end of interview."

Rice was the starting quarterback on the Irish's 1988 national championship and Foley was thought to be headed for a lucrative career in the NFL before suffering a career-ending injury. Both student-athletes graduated from the prestigious school. Rice, Foley and former basketball player Keith Robinson, who also graduated, are the only Proposition 48 student-athletes Notre Dame has ever accepted.

Then there's also the not-so-happy case of former high school football All-American Alcindor Coleman of Rochester, New York, a 1990 graduate. Coleman, a 6-foot-4, 300-pound lineman signed with the University of Pittsburgh in February 1990, but didn't score high enough on his SAT. Pittsburgh prepared to enroll Coleman into a Pennsylvania prep school if he didn't qualify academically but Coleman didn't like that option and enrolled at a Texas junior college. After a year at the juco, Coleman left and never played a minute of Division I football.

Yes, the future appears to be pointing toward stronger academic standards and it could hit more coaches where it hurts the most—in their pockets.

It is apparent that all schools have the ability to graduate student-athletes. Yet some schools are disillusioned with the "student" in the word "student-athlete," and concentrate merely on the "athlete," the ones who bring in millions of dollars to the university. It is important for the student-athlete to find the right school which cares about academics as well as athletics. Some graduation rates for 1993 NCAA Division I programs are listed at the end of this chapter. For additional information regarding Proposition 48 and the NCAA's graduation rates, please contact the NCAA.

## Conclusion

Academics should be first and foremost on the student-athlete's mind but often times they are not. If student-athletes would take as much time preparing academically as they do preparing athletically before and during college, the institutions ridiculously low graduation rates would improve greatly.

By combining the wonderful world of academics and athletics, a special magic is created. Take a moment and think about how many people you know who have gone off to college and participated in athletes. What the colleges are doing is giving you the opportunity to continue something you enjoy and *pay* for your college degree—if you take advantage of it. Student-athletes should have a degree to fall back on because many will not get the opportunity to play professionally. That's fact, not fiction. A college educated student-athlete has a much better chance of being productive in the real world than one who isn't.

It all begins with selecting the right college—to see a dream come into sharper focus. A student-athlete should choose a college that concentrates not only on athletics but academics as well. I'm rather confident that by following this book carefully, a student-athlete will be able to handle the pressures of recruiting. Student-athletes who possess the potential to earn a college scholarship are among a privileged few and are indeed special people.

Handling the recruiting process is *not* a simple task. Then again, nothing in life that is worth anything ever is. After reading this book the student-athlete, parents and coaches will know how to play the sports recruiting game. And win.

Universities & Colleges

For athletic scholarship information, call the numbers listed below:

# Alabama

**Alabama Agricultural and Mechanical University**
Normal, AL 35762
(205) 851-5000
African-American undergraduate student body: 93 percent

**Alabama State University**
915 S. Jackson Street
Montgomery, AL 36101
(334) 229-4291
African-American undergraduate student body: 97 percent

**Auburn University**
202 Martin Hall
Auburn University, AL 36849
(334) 844-4080
African-American undergraduate student body: six percent

**Jacksonville State University**
700 Pelham Road N.
Jacksonville, AL 36265
(205) 782-5400
African-American undergraduate student body: 16 percent

**Miles College**
Fairfield, AL 35064
(205) 923-2771
African-American undergraduate student body: 93 percent

**Samford University**
800 Lakeshore Drive
Birmingham, AL 35229
(800) 888-7218
African-American undergraduate student body: five percent

**Selma University**
Selma, AL 36701
(334) 872-2533
African-American undergraduate student body: 94 percent

**Stillman College**
Tuscaloosa, AL 35403
(205) 349-4240
African-American undergraduate student body: 97 percent

**Talladega College**
627 W. Battle Street
Talladega, AL 35160
(205) 761-6219
African-American undergraduate student body: 100 percent

**Troy State University**
University Avenue
Troy, AL 36082
(334) 670-3179
African-American undergraduate
student body: 18 percent

**Tuskegee University**
1506 Franklin Road
Tuskegee, AL 36088
(334) 727-8500
African-American undergraduate
student body: 94 percent

**University of Alabama**
Box 870132
Tuscaloosa, AL 35487
(205) 348-5666
African-American undergraduate
student body: 12 percent

**University of Alabama-Birmingham**
UAB Station
Birmingham, AL 35294
(205) 934-8221
African-American undergraduate
student body: 25 percent

**University of South Alabama**
307 University Boulevard
Mobile, AL 36688
(334) 460-6141
African-American undergraduate
student body: 11 percent

# Arizona

**Arizona State University**
Tempe, AZ 85287
(602) 965-7788
African-American undergraduate
student body: three percent

**Northern Arizona University**
PO Box 4084
Flagstaff, AZ 86011
(520) 523-5511
African-American undergraduate
student body: one percent

**University of Arizona**
Tucson, AZ 85721
(520) 621-3237
African-American undergraduate
student body: three percent

# Arkansas

**Arkansas Baptist College**
Little Rock, AR 72202
(501) 374-7856
African-American undergraduate
student body: 98 percent

**Arkansas State University**
PO box 1630
State University, AR 72467
(501) 972-3024
African-American undergraduate
student body: 10 percent

**Philander Smith College**
Little Rock, AR 72202
(501) 375-9845
African-American undergraduate
student body: 90 percent

**University of Arkansas-Fayetteville**
200 Silas Hunt Hall
Fayetteville, AR 72701
(800) 377-8632
African-American undergraduate
student body: six percent

**University of Arkansas-Little Rock**
2801 S. University Avenue
Little Rock, AR 72204
(501) 569-3127
African-American undergraduate
student body: 21 percent

**University of Arkansas at Pine Bluff**
Pine Bluff, AR 71601-2799
(501) 543-8000
African-American undergraduate
student body: 85 percent

# California

**Fresno State**
5150 N Maple
Fresno, CA 93740
(209) 278-2261
African-American undergraduate
student body: six percent

**Cal State-Fullerton**
800 N. State College Boulevard
Fullerton, CA 92834
(714) 278-2370
African-American undergraduate
student body: three percent

**Long Beach State**
1350 Bellflower Boulevard
Long Beach, CA 90840
(562) 985-5471
African-American undergraduate
student body: nine percent

**Cal State Northridge**
18111 Nordhoff Street
Northridge, CA 91330
(818) 677-3700
African-American undergraduate
student body: nine percent

**Cal State San Luis Obispo**
San Luis Obispo, CA 93407
(805) 756-2311
African-American undergraduate
student body: two percent

**Sacramento State**
6000 J Street
Sacramento, CA 95819
(916) 278-3901
African-American undergraduate
student body: seven percent

**Loyola Marymount University**
7900 Loyola Boulevard
Los Angeles, CA 90045
(310) 338-2750
African-American undergraduate
student body: eight percent

**Mount St. Mary's College**
12001 Chalon Road
Los Angeles, CA 90049
(310) 954-4250
African-American undergraduate
student body: 10 percent

**Pepperdine University**
24255 Pacific Coast Highway
Malibu, CA 90263
(310) 456-4392
African-American undergraduate
student body: five percent

**San Diego State**
5500 Campanile Drive
San Diego, CA 92182
(619) 594-6871
African-American undergraduate
student body: five percent

**San Jose State University**
1 Washington Square
San Jose, CA 95192
(408) 283-7500
African-American undergraduate
student body: five percent

**Santa Clara University**
500 El Camino Real
Santa Clara, CA 95053
(408) 554-4700
African-American undergraduate
student body: three percent

**Stanford University**
Old Union Room 232
Stanford, CA 94305
(415) 723-2091
African-American undergraduate
student body: eight percent

**University of California-Berkeley**
110 Sproul Hall
Berkeley, CA 94720
(510) 642-3175
African-American undergraduate
student body: six percent

**University of Cal-Irvine**
Irvine, CA 92697
(714) 824-6703
African-American undergraduate
student body: two percent

**UCLA**
405 Hilgard Avenue
Los Angeles, CA 90095
(310) 825-3101
African-American undergraduate
student body: six percent

**University of Cal-Santa Barbara**
Santa Barbara, CA 93106
(805) 893-2485
African-American undergraduate
student body: three percent

**University of San Diego**
5998 Alcala Park
San Diego, CA 92110
(619) 260-4506
African-American undergraduate
student body: three percent

**University of San Francisco**
Ignatian Heights
San Francisco, CA 94117
(415) 422-6563
African-American undergraduate
student body: five percent

**USC**
University Park
Los Angeles, CA 90089
(213) 740-1111
African-American undergraduate
student body: six percent

**University of the Pacific**
3601 Pacific Avenue
Stockton, CA 95211
(800) 959-2867
African-American undergraduate
student body: three percent

# Colorado

**Colorado State University**
Fort Collins, CO 80523
(970) 491-6909
African-American undergraduate
student body: one percent

**United States Air Force Academy**
HQ USAFA/RRS
2304 Cadet Drive
Suite 200
USAF Academy, CO 80840
(719) 333-3070
African-American undergraduate
student body: five percent

**University of Colorado**
Regent Admin. Center
Room 125
Campus Box 6
Boulder, CO 80309
(303) 492-6301
African-American undergraduate
student body: two percent

# Connecticut

**Central Connecticut State University**
1615 Stanley Street
New Britain, CT 06050
(860) 832-2278
African-American undergraduate
student body: seven percent

**Fairfield University**
1073 N. Benson Road
Fairfield, CT 06430
(203) 254-4100
African-American undergraduate
student body: three percent

**University of Connecti**cut
2131 Hillside Road, U-88
Storrs, CT 06269
(860) 486-3137
African-American undergraduate
student body: four percent

**University of Hartford**
200 Bloomfield Avenue
West Hartford, CT 06117
(860) 768-4296
African-American undergraduate
student body: six percent

**Yale University**
PO box 208234
New Haven, CT 06520
(203) 432-9300
African-American undergraduate
student body: eight percent

# Delaware

**University of Delaware**
USPS 077580
Newark, DE 19716
(302) 831-8123
African-American undergraduate
student body: six percent

**Delaware State University**
1200 N. Dupont Highway
Dover, DE 19901
(302) 739-4917
African-American undergraduate
student body: N/A

# District of Columbia

**American University**
4400 Massachusetts Avenue, N.W.
Washington, DC 20016
(202) 885-6000
African-American undergraduate
student body: seven percent

**Georgetown University**
37th and O Streets N.W.
Washington, DC 20057
(202) 687-3600
African-American undergraduate
student body: six percent

**George Washington University**
2121 Eye Street, N.W.
Washington, DC 20052
(202) 994-6040
African-American undergraduate
student body: seven percent

**Howard University**
2400 Sixth Street, N.W.
Washington, DC 20059
(202) 806-2763
African-American undergraduate
student body: 90 percent

**University of the District of Columbia**
4200 Connecticut Avenue, N.W.
Washington, DC 20008
(202) 274-5010
African-American undergraduate
student body: 72 percent

# Florida

**Bethune-Cookman College**
640 Dr. Mary McLeod Bethune
Boulevard
Daytona Beach, FL 32114
(800) 448-0228
African-American undergraduate
student body: 93 percent

**Edward Waters College**
Jacksonville, FL 32209
(904) 366-2506
African-American undergraduate
student body: 94 percent

**Florida A&M University**
Tallahassee, FL 32307
(904) 599-3796
African-American undergraduate
student body: 93 percent

**Florida Atlantic University**
PO Box 3091
Boca Raton, FL 33431
(561) 367-3040
African-American undergraduate
student body: 11 percent

**Florida International University**
University Park
Miami, FL 33199
(305) 348-2363
African-American undergraduate
student body: 15 percent

**Florida Memorial College**
Miami, FL 33054
(800) 822-1362
African-American undergraduate
student body: 87 percent

**Florida State University**
Tallahassee, FL 32206
(904) 644-6200
African-American undergraduate
student body: 10 percent

**Jacksonville University**
2800 University Boulevard N.
Jacksonville, FL 32211
(904) 745-7000
African-American undergraduate
student body: 10 percent

**Stetson University**
421 N. Woodland Boulevard
Deland, FL 32720
(800) 688-0101
African-American undergraduate
student body: three percent

**University of Central Florida**
4000 Central Florida Boulevard
Orlando, FL 32816
(407) 823-3000
African-American undergraduate
student body: seven percent

**University of Florida**
201 Criser Hall
Gainesville, FL 32611
(352) 392-1365
African-American undergraduate
student body: six percent

**University of Miami**
PO Box 248025
Coral Gables, FL 33124
(305) 284-4323
African-American undergraduate
student body: 11 percent

**University of South Florida**
4202 E. Fowler Avenue
Tampa, FL 33620
(813) 974-3350
African-American undergraduate
student body: 10 percent

# Georgia

**Albany State University**
504 College Drive
Albany, GA 31705
(912) 430-4646
African-American undergraduate
student body: 93 percent

**Clark Atlanta University**
James P. Brawley Drive at Fair
Street
Atlanta, GA 30314
(404) 880-8784
African-American undergraduate
student body: 100 percent

**Fort Valley State College**
Fort Valley, GA 31030
(912) 825-6211
African-American undergraduate
student body: N/A

**Georgia Tech**
225 North Avenue N.W.
Atlanta, GA 30332
(404) 894-4154
African-American undergraduate
student body: nine percent

**Georgia Southern University**
Landrum Box 8027
Statesboro, GA 30460
(912) 681-5531
African-American undergraduate
student body: 27 percent

**Georgia State University**
University Plaza
Atlanta, GA 30303
(404) 651-2365
African-American undergraduate
student body: N/A

**Mercer University**
1400 Coleman Avenue
Macon, GA 31207
(912) 752-2650
African-American undergraduate
student body: 19 percent

**Morehouse College**
830 Westview Drive S.W.
Atlanta, GA 30314
(800) 851-1254
African-American undergraduate
student body: 99 percent

**Morris Brown College**
Atlanta, GA 30314
(404) 220-0270
African-American undergraduate
student body: 98 percent

**Paine College**
Augusta, GA 30910
(706) 821-8200
African-American undergraduate
student body: 98 percent

**Savannah State College**
Savannah, GA 31404
(912) 356-2186
African-American undergraduate
student body: 92 percent

**Spelman College**
350 Spelman Lane, S.W.
Atlanta, GA 30314
(800) 982-2411
African-American undergraduate
student body: 95 percent

**University of Georgia**
212 Terrell Hall
Athens, GA 30602
(706) 542-2112
African-American undergraduate
student body: seven percent

# Hawaii

**University of Hawaii**
2600 Campus Road
Honolulu, HI 96822
(808) 956-8975
African-American undergraduate
student body: one percent

# Idaho

**Boise State University**
1910 University Drive
Boise, ID 83725
(208) 385-1156
African-American undergraduate
student body: one percent

**Idaho State University**
741 S. Seventh Avenue
Pocatello, ID 83209
(208) 236-2475
African-American undergraduate
student body: one percent

**University of Idaho**
Moscow, ID 83844
(208) 885-6326
African-American undergraduate
student body: one percent

# Illinois

**Bradley University**
1501 W. Bradley Avenue
Peoria, IL 61625
(800) 447-6460
African-American undergraduate
student body: five percent

**Chicago State University**
9501 S. King Drive
Chicago, IL 60628
(773) 995-2513
African-American undergraduate
student body: 92 percent

**DePaul University**
1 E. Jackson Boulevard
Chicago, IL 60604
(312) 362-8300
African-American undergraduate
student body: 13 percent

**Eastern Illinois University**
600 Lincoln Avenue
Charleston, IL 61920
(800) 252-5711
African-American undergraduate
student body: five percent

**Illinois State University**
2200 Admissions
Normal, IL 61790
(309) 438-2181
African-American undergraduate
student body: nine percent

**Loyola University-Chicago**
820 N. Michigan Avenue
Chicago, IL 60611
(312) 915-6500
African-American undergraduate
student body: seven percent

**Northeastern Illinois University**
5500 N. Saint Louis Avenue
Chicago, IL 60625
(773) 794-2600
African-American undergraduate
student body: 13 percent

**Northern Illinois University**
PO Box 3001
DeKalb, IL 60115
(815) 753-0446
African-American undergraduate
student body: 10 percent

**Northwestern University**
PO Box 3060
1801 Hinman Avenue
Evanston, IL 60204
(847) 491-7271
African-American undergraduate
student body: six percent

**Southern Illinois University**
Mail Code 4701
Carbondale, IL 62901
(618) 453-4381
African-American undergraduate
student body: 14 percent

**University of Illinois-Chicago**
601 S. Morgan M/C 102
Chicago, IL 60607
(312) 996-4350
African-American undergraduate
student body: 10 percent

**University of Illinois**
506 S. Wright Street
Urbana, IL 61801
(217) 333-0302
African-American undergraduate
student body: seven percent

**Western Illinois University**
1 University Circle
Macomb, IL 61455
(309) 298-3157
African-American undergraduate
student body: eight percent

# Indiana

**Ball State University**
2000 University Avenue
Muncie, IN 47306
(765) 285-8300
African-American undergraduate
student body: five percent

**Butler University**
4600 Sunset Avenue
Indianapolis, IN 46208
(317) 940-8100
African-American undergraduate
student body: four percent

**Indiana State University**
210 N. Seventh Street
Terre Haute, IN 47809
(800) 742-0891
African-American undergraduate
student body: eight percent

**Indiana University**
300 N. Jordan Avenue
Bloomington, IN 47405
(812) 855-0661
African-American undergraduate
student body: four percent

**Notre Dame**
Room 113, Main Building
Notre Dame, IN 46556
(219) 631-7505
African-American undergraduate
student body: three percent

**University of Evansville**
1800 Lincoln Avenue
Evansville, IN 47722
(812) 479-2468
African-American undergraduate
student body: three percent

**Valparaiso University**
Valparaiso, IN 46383
(888) 468-2576
African-American undergraduate
student body: four percent

# Iowa

**Drake University**
2507 University Avenue
Des Moines, IA 50311
(800) 443-7253
African-American undergraduate
student body: four percent

**Iowa State University**
100 Alumni Hall
Ames, IA 50011
(800) 262-3810
African-American undergraduate
student body: three percent

**University of Iowa**
107 Calvin Hall
Iowa City, IA 52242
(319) 335-3847
African-American undergraduate
student body: two percent

**University of Northern Iowa**
1222 W. 27th Street
Cedar Falls, IA 50614
(800) 772-2037
African-American undergraduate
student body: two percent

# Kansas

**Kansas State University**
Anderson Hall
Manhattan, KS 66506
(916) 532-6250
African-American undergraduate
student body: three percent

**University of Kansas**
126 Strong Hall
Lawrence, KS 66045
(913) 864-3911
African-American undergraduate
student body: three percent

**Wichita State University**
1845 Fairmount
Wichita, KS 67260
(316) 978-3085
African-American undergraduate
student body: six percent

# Kentucky

**Eastern Kentucky**
Lancaster Avenue
Richmond, KY 40475
(606) 622-2106
African-American undergraduate
student body: N/A

**Kentucky State University**
East Main Street
Frankfort, KY 40601
(800) 325-1716
African-American undergraduate
student body: 57 percent

**Morehead State University**
HM 301
Morehead, KY 40351
(606) 783-2000
African-American undergraduate
student body: three percent

**Murray State University**
15th and Main Streets
Murray, KY 42071
(502) 762-3741
African-American undergraduate
student body: six percent

**University of Kentucky**
206 Administration Building
Lexington, KY 40506
(606) 257-2000
African-American undergraduate
student body: five percent

**University of Louisville**
Office of Admissions
Louisville, KY 40292
(502) 852-6531
African-American undergraduate
student body: 14 percent

**Western Kentucky University**
1 Big Red Way
Bowling Green, KY 42101
(502) 745-2551
African-American undergraduate
student body: four percent

# Louisiana

**Centenary College**
PO Box 41188
Shreveport, LA 71134
(318) 869-5131
African-American undergraduate
student body: four percent

**Dillard University**
New Orleans, LA 70122
(504) 283-8822
African-American undergraduate
student body: 97 percent

**Grambling State University**
Box 607
Grambling, LA 71245
(318) 274-6183
African-American undergraduate
student body: 96 percent

**Lousiana State University-Baton Rouge**
110 Thomas Boyd Hall
Baton Rouge, LA 70803
(504) 388-1175
African-American undergraduate
student body: eight percent

**Louisiana Tech University**
Box 3178
Tech Station
Ruston, LA 71272
(318) 257-3036
African-American undergraduate
student body: 13 percent

**McNeese State University**
Ryan Street
Lake Charles, LA 70609
(318) 475-5146
African-American undergraduate
student body: 16 percent

**Nicholls State University**
PO Box 2004
University Station
Thibodaux, LA 70310
(504) 448-4145
African-American undergraduate
student body: 14 percent

**Northeast Louisiana University**
700 University Avenue
Monroe, LA 71209
(318) 342-5252
African-American undergraduate
student body: 22 percent

**Northwestern State**
Natchitoches, LA
(318) 357-4503
African-American undergraduate
student body: 24 percent

**Southern University and A&M College**
Southern Branch PO
Baton Rouge, LA 70813
(504) 771-2430
African-American undergraduate
student body: N/A

**Southern University-New Orleans**
6400 Press Drive
New Orleans, LA 70126
(504) 286-5314
African-American undergraduate
student body: N/A

**Tulane University**
6823 St. Charles Avenue
Room 210 Gibson Hall
New Orleans, LA 70118
(504) 865-5731
African-American undergraduate
student body: nine percent

**Southeastern Louisiana University**
SLU 752
Hammond, LA 70402
(504) 549-2066
African-American undergraduate
student body: nine percent

**Southwestern Louisiana**
University Avenue
Lafayette, LA 70504
(318) 482-6467
African-American undergraduate
student body: 20 percent

**University of New Orleans**
Lake Front
New Orleans, LA 70148
(504) 280-6595
African-American undergraduate
student body: 18 percent

**Xavier University of Louisiana**
7325 Palmetto Street
New Orleans, LA 70125
(504) 483-7388
African-American undergraduate
student body: 93 percent

# Maryland

**Bowie State University**
14000 Jericho Park Road
Bowie, MD 20715
(301) 464-6570
African-American undergraduate
student body: 83 percent

**Coppin State College**
2500 W. North Avenue
Baltimore, MD 21216
(410) 383-5990
African-American undergraduate
student body: 95 percent

**Loyola College**
4501 N. Charles Street
Baltimore, MD 21210
(410) 617-5012
African-American undergraduate
student body: four percent

**Morgan State University**
1700 E. Cold Spring Lane
Baltimore, MD 21251
(410) 319-3000
African-American undergraduate
student body: 95 percent

**Mount St. Mary's College**
16300 Old Emmitsburg Road
Emmitsburg, MD 21727
(800) 448-4347
African-American undergraduate
student body: five percent

**Towson State University**
8000 York Road
Towson, MD 21252
(410) 830-3333
African-American undergraduate
student body: nine percent

**United States Naval Academy**
117 Decatur Road
Annapolis, MD 21402
(410) 293-4361
African-American undergraduate
student body: seven percent

**University of Maryland**
College Park, MD 20742
(301) 314-8385
African-American undergraduate
student body: 14 percent

**University of Maryland
Baltimore County**
1000 Hilltop Circle
Baltimore, MD 21250
(410) 455-2291
African-American undergraduate
student body: N/A

**University of Maryland-Eastern
Shore**
J.T. Williams Hall
Room 2106
Princess Anne, MD 21853
(410) 651-6410
African-American undergraduate
student body: 76 percent

# Massachusetts

**Boston College**
140 Commonwealth Avenue
Chestnut Hill, MA 02167
(617) 552-3100
African-American undergraduate
student body: four percent

**Boston University**
121 Bay State Road
Boston, MA 02215
(617) 353-2300
African-American undergraduate
student body: N/A

**Harvard University**
Undergraduate Admissions Office
8 Garden Street, Byerly Hall
Cambridge, MA 02138
(617) 495-1551
African-American undergraduate
student body: eight percent

**Holy Cross**
College Street
Worchester, MA 01610
(508) 793-2443
African-American undergraduate
student body: three percent

**Northeastern University**
360 Huntington Avenue
Boston, MA 02115
(617) 373-2200
African-American undergraduate
student body: five percent

**University of Massachusetts**
Admissions Center
Amherst, MA 01003
(413) 545-0222
African-American undergraduate
student body: five percent

# Michigan

**Central Michigan University**
105 Warriner
Mount Pleasant, MI 48859
(517) 774-3076
African-American undergraduate
student body: four percent

**Eastern Michigan University**
PO Box 91
Ypsilanti, MI 48197
(313) 487-3063
African-American undergraduate
student body: 14 percent

**Michigan State University**
Room 250
Administration Building
East Lansing, MI 48824
(517) 355-8332
African-American undergraduate
student body: eight percent

**University of Detroit-Mercy**
PO Box 19900
Detroit, MI 48219
(313) 993-1245
African-American undergraduate
student body: 38 percent

**University of Michigan**
1220 Student Activities Bldg.
Office of Undergraduate Admissions
Ann Arbor, MI 48109
(313) 764-7433
African-American undergraduate
student body: nine percent

**Western Michigan University**
Kalamazoo, MI 49008
(616) 387-2000
African-American undergraduate
student body: seven percent

# Minnesota

**University of Minnesota**
231 Pillsbury Drive S.E.
Minneapolis, MN 55455
(612) 625-2008
African-American undergraduate
student body: four percent

# Mississippi

**Alcorn State**
1000 ASU Drive #300
Lorman, MS 39096
(601) 877-6147
African-American undergraduate
student body: 97 percent

**Jackson State**
1400 J.R. Lynch Street
Jackson, MS 39217
(601) 968-2100
African-American undergraduate
student body: 97 percent

**Mississippi State**
PO Box 5268
Mississippi State, MS 39762
(601) 325-2224
African-American undergraduate
student body: 16 percent

**Mississippi Valley State**
14000 Highway 82 W.
Itta Bena, MS 38941
(601) 254-3344
African-American undergraduate
student body: 98 percent

**Rust College**
Holly Springs, MS 38635
(601) 252-8000
African-American undergraduate
student body: 94 percent

**Tougaloo College**
500 W. County Line Road
Tougaloo, MS 39174
(601) 977-7764
African-American undergraduate
studenty body: 100 percent

**University of Mississippi**
University, MS 38677
(601) 232-7226
African-American undergraduate
student body: 10 percent

**University of Southern Mississippi**
Box 5167 Southern Station
Hattiesburg, MS 39406
(601) 266-5000
African-American undergraduate
student body: 20 percent

# Missouri

**Harris-Stowe State College**
St. Louis, MO 63103
(314) 533-3366
African-American undergraduate
student body: 65 percent

**Lincoln University**
Jefferson City, MO 65102-0029
(314) 681-5000
African-American undergraduate
student body: 28 percent

**St. Louis University**
221 N. Grand Boulevard
St. Louis, MO 63103
(314) 977-2500
African-American undergraduate
student body: nine percent

**Southeast Missouri State**
901 S. National
Springfield, MO 65804
(800) 492-7900
African-American undergraduate
student body: two percent

**University of Missouri**
305 Jesse Hall
Columbia, MO 65211
(573) 882-7786
African-American undergraduate
student body: six percent

**University of Missouri-Kansas City**
5100 Rockhill Road
Kansas City, MO 64110
(816) 235-1111
African-American undergraduate
student body: 10 percent

# Montana

**Montana State University**
113 Hamilton Hall or
PO Box 172190
Bozeman, MT 59717
(406) 994-2452
African-American undergraduate
student body: 0 percent

**University of Montana**
101 Lodge, U of M
Missoula, MT 59812
(406) 243-6266
African-American undergraduate
student body: 0 percent

# Nebraska

**Creighton University**
2500 California Plaza
Omaha, NE 68178
(800) 282-5835
African-American undergraduate
student body: four percent

**University of Nebraska**
14th and R Streets
Lincoln, NE 68588
(800) 742-8800
African-American undergraduate
student body: two percent

# Nevada

**UNLV**
4505 S. Maryland Parkway
Las Vegas, NV 89154
(702) 895-3443
African-American undergraduate
student body: seven percent

**University of Nevada-Reno**
Reno, NV 89557
(702) 784-6865
African-American undergraduate
student body: two percent

# New Hampshire

**Dartmouth College**
6016 McNutt Hall
Hanover, NH 03755
(603) 646-2875
African-American undergraduate
student body: five percent

**University of New Hampshire**
4 Garrison Avenue
Durham, NH 03824
(603) 862-1360
African-American undergraduate
student body: one percent

# New Jersey

**Fairleigh Dickinson University**
1000 River Road
Teaneck, NJ 07666
(800) 338-8803
African-American undergraduate
student body: 10 percent

**Monmouth University**
Norwood and Cedar Avenues
W. Long Beach, NJ 07764
(800) 543-9671
African-American undergraduate
student body: five percent

**Princeton University**
Box 430
Princeton, NJ 08544
(609) 258-3060
African-American undergraduate
student body: seven percent

**Rider University**
2083 Lawrenceville Road
Lawrenceville, NJ 08648
(609) 896-5042
African-American undergraduate
student body: seven percent

**Rutgers University**
PO Box 2101
New Brunswick, NJ 08903
(908) 445-3777
African-American undergraduate
student body: eight percent

**Seton Hall**
400 S. Orange Avenue
South Orange, NJ 07079
(201) 761-9332
African-American undergraduate
student body: 13 percent

**St. Peter's College**
2641 Kennedy Boulevard
Jersey City, NJ 07306
(201) 915-9213
African-American undergraduate
student body: 14 percent

# New Mexico

**New Mexico State**
Box 30001
Department 3A
Las Cruces, NM 88003
(505) 646-3121
African-American undergraduate
student body: two percent

**University of New Mexico**
Student Services Center #253
Albuquerque, NM 87131
(505) 277-2446
African-American undergraduate
student body: three percent

# New York

**Canisius College**
2001 Main Street
Buffalo, NY 14208
(800) 843-1517
African-American undergraduate
student body: six percent

**City University of New York,
Medgar Evers College**
Brooklyn, NY 11225
(718) 270-4900
African-American undergraduate
student body: 91 percent

**City University of New York, New York City**
Brooklyn, NY 11201-2983
(718) 260-5000
African-American undergraduate
student body: 51 percent

**City University of New York, York College**
Jamaica, NY 11225
(718) 262-2000
African-American undergraduate
student body: 62 percent

**Colgate University**
13 Oak Drive
Hamilton, NY 13346
(315) 824-7401
African-American undergraduate
student body: four percent

**Columbia University**
212 Hamilton Hall
New York, NY 10027
(212) 854-2521
African-American undergraduate
student body: eight percent

**Cornell University**
410 Thurston Avenue
Ithaca, NY 14850
(607) 255-5241
African-American undergraduate
student body: four percent

**Fordham University**
113 W. 60th Street
New York, NY 10458
(800) 367-3426
African-American undergraduate
student body: six percent

**Hofstra University**
100 Hofstra University
Hempstead, NY 11550
(516) 463-6700
African-American undergraduate
student body: five percent

**Iona College**
715 North Avenue
New Rochelle, NY 10801
(914) 633-2502
African-American undergraduate
student body: 14 percent

**Long Island University**
1 University Plaza
Brooklyn, NY 11201
(718) 488-1011
African-American undergraduate
student body: 42 percent

**Manhattan College**
Manhattan College Parkway
Riverdale, NY 10471
(718) 862-7200
African-American undergraduate
student body: seven percent

**Marist College**
North Road
Poughkeepsie, NY 12601
(914) 575-3226
African-American undergraduate
student body: six percent

**Niagara University**
Niagara University, NY 14109
(716) 286-8700
African-American undergraduate
student body: five percent

**Siena College**
515 Loudon Road
Loudonville, NY 12211
(800) 457-4362
African-American undergraduate
student body: two percent

**St. Bonaventure**
PO Box D
St. Bonaventure, NY 14778
(800) 462-5050
African-American undergraduate
student body: one percent

**St. Francis College**
180 Remsen Street
Brooklyn, NY 11201
(718) 522-2300
African-American undergraduate
student body: 24 percent

**St. John's University**
8000 Utopia Parkway
Jamaica, NY 11439
(718) 990-6114
African-American undergraduate
student body: 12 percent

**Syracuse University**
201 Tolley Administration Building
Syracuse, NY 13244
(315) 443-3611
African-American undergraduate
student body: seven percent

**United State Military Academy**
600 Thayer Road
West Point, NY 10996
(914) 938-4041
African-American undergraduate
student body: six percent

**University of Buffalo**
17 Capen Hall
Buffalo, NY 14260
(716) 645-6900
African-American undergraduate
student body: seven percent

**Wagner College**
631 Howard Avenue
Staten Island, NY 10301
(718) 390-3411
African-American undergraduate
student body: six percent

# North Carolina

**Appalachian State University**
Boone, NC 28608
(704) 262-2120
African-American undergraduate
student body: three percent

**Bennett College**
Greensboro, NC 27401
(910) 273-4431
African-American undergraduate
student body: 99 percent

**Campbell University**
PO Box 546
Buies, NC 27506
(800) 334-4111
African-American undergraduate
student body: N/A

**Davidson College**
PO Box 1719
Davidson, NC 28036
(704) 892-2230
African-American undergraduate
student body: 93 percent

**Duke University**
2138 Campus Drive
Box 90586
Durham, NC 27708
(919) 684-3214
African-American undergraduate
student body: eight percent

**East Carolina University**
Fifth Street
Greenville, NC 27856
(919) 328-6640
African-American undergraduate
student body: 11 percent

**Elizabeth City State University**
1704 Weeksville Road
Elizabeth City, NC 27909
African-American undergraduate
student body: 74 percent

**Fayetteville State University**
Newbold Station
Fayetteville, NC 28301
(910) 486-1371
African-American undergraduate
student body: 72 percent

**Johnson C. Smith University**
100 Beatties Ford Road
Charlotte, NC 28216
(704) 378-1010
African-American undergraduate
student body: 100 percent

**Livingstone College**
Salisbury, NC 28144
(704) 638-5500
African-American undergraduate
student body: 90 percent

**North Carolina A&T State University**
1601 E. Market Street
Greensboro, NC 27411
(910) 334-7946
African-American undergraduate
student body: 92 percent

**North Carolina Central University**
Fayetteville Street
Durham, NC 27707
(919) 560-6080
African-American undergraduate
student body: 92 percent

**North Carolina State**
Box 7001
Raleigh, NC 27695
(919) 515-2434
African-American undergraduate
student body: 10 percent

**Shaw University**
118 E. South Street
Raleigh, NC 27601
(919) 546-8275
African-American undergraduate
student body: 96 percent

**St. Augustine's College**
1315 Oakwood Avenue
Raleigh, NC 27610
(919) 516-4016
African-American undergraduate
student body: 91 percent

**North Carolina-Asheville**
1 University Heights
Asheville, NC 28804
(704) 251-6481
African-American undergraduate
student body: four percent

**University of North Carolina**
Jackson Hall
UADM CB# 2200
Chapel Hill, NC 27599
(919) 966-3621
African-American undergraduate
student body: 11 percent

**University of North Carolina-Charlotte**
9201 University City Boulevard
Charlotte, NC 28223
(704) 547-2213
African-American undergraduate
student body: 16 percent

**University of North Carolina-Greensboro**
1000 Spring Garden Street
Greensboro, NC 27412
(910) 334-5243
African-American undergraduate
student body: 15

**University of North Carolina-Wilmington**
601 S. College Road
Wilmington, NC 28403
(910) 962-3243
African-American undergraduate
student body: six percent

**Wake Forest University**
PO Box 7265
Raleigh, NC 27109
(910) 759-5201
African-American undergraduate
student body: eight percent

**Western Carolina University**
Cullowhee, NC 28723
(704) 227-7317
African-American undergraduate
student body: five percent

**Winston-Salem State University**
601 Martin Luther King Jr., Drive
Winston-Salem, NC 27110
(910) 750-2070
African-American undergraduate
student body: 79 percent

# Ohio

**Bowling Green State University**
110 McFail Center
Bowling Green, Ohio 43403
(419) 372-2086
African-American undergraduate
student body: three percent

**Central State University**
1400 Brush Row Road
Wilberforce, Ohio 45384
(937) 376-6348
African-American undergraduate
student body: 100 percent

**Cleveland State University**
E. 24th and Euclid Avenue
Cleveland, Ohio 44115
(216) 687-3754
African-American undergraduate
student body: 18 percent

**Kent State University**
PO Box 5190
Kent, Ohio 44242
(330) 672-2444
African-American undergraduate
student body: seven percent

**Miami University**
Oxford, Ohio 45056
(513) 529-2531
African-American undergraduate
student body: three percent

**Ohio State**
Third Floor Lincoln Tower
1800 Cannon Drive
Columbus, Ohio 43210
(614) 292-3980
African-American undergraduate
student body: seven percent

**Ohio University**
Athens, Ohio 45701
(614) 593-4100
African-American undergraduate
student body: four percent

**University of Akron**
302 Buchtel Common
Akron, Ohio 44325
(330) 972-7100
African-American undergraduate
student body: 13 percent

**University of Cincinnati**
Enrollment Services
PO Box 0091
Cincinnati, Ohio 45221
(513) 556-1100
African-American undergraduate
student body: nine percent

**University of Dayton**
300 College Park Drive
Dayton, Ohio 45469
(937) 229-4411
African-American undergraduate
student body: three percent

**University of Toledo**
2801 W. Bancroft
Toledo, Ohio 43606
(419) 530-8888
African-American undergraduate
student body: 13 percent

**Wilberforce University**
1055 N. Bickett Road
Wilberforce, Ohio 45384
(800) 367-8568
African-American undergraduate
student body: 100 percent

**Wright State University**
3640 Colonel Glenn Highway
Dayton, Ohio 45435
(937) 775-5700
African-American undergraduate
student body: nine percent

**Xavier University**
3800 Victory Parkway
Cincinnati, Ohio 45207
(513) 745-3301
African-American undergraduate
student body: eight percent

**Youngstown University**
One University Plaza
Youngstown, Ohio 44555
(330) 742-3150
African-American undergraduate
student body: eight percent

# Oklahoma

**Langston University**
Laangston, OK 73050
(405) 466-2231
African-American undergraduate
student body: 75 percent

**Oklahoma State University**
104 Whitehurst Hall
Stillwater, OK 74078
(405) 744-5000
African-American undergraduate
student body: two percent

**Oral Roberts University**
7777 S. Lewis
Tulsa, OK 74171
(918) 495-6518
African-American undergraduate
student body: 21 percent

**University of Oklahoma**
1000 Asp Avenue
Norman, OK 73019
(405) 325-2251
African-American undergraduate
student body: seven percent

**University of Tulsa**
600 S. College Avenue
Tulsa, OK 74104
(918) 631-2307
African-American undergraduate
student body: seven percent

## Oregon

**Oregon State University**
104 Kerr Administration Building
Corvallis, OR 97331
(541) 737-4411
African-American undergraduate
student body: one percent

**Portland State University**
PO Box 751
Portland, OR 97207
(503) 725-3511
African-American undergraduate
student body: three percent

**University of Oregon**
1217 University of Oregon
Eugene, OR 97403
(503) 232-3825
African-American undergraduate
student body: one percent

**University of Portland**
5000 N. Willamette Boulevard
Portland, OR 97203
(503) 283-7147
African-American undergraduate
student body: one percent

## Pennsylvania

**Bucknell University**
Lewisburg, PA 17837
(717) 524-1101
African-American undergraduate
student body: three percent

**Cheyney University**
Cheyney and Creek Roads
Cheyney, PA 19319
(610) 399-2275
African-American undergraduate
student body: 97 percent

**Drexel University**
32nd and Chestnut Streets
Philadelphia, PA 19104
(800) 237-3935
African-American undergraduate
student body: 10 percent

**Duquesne University**
600 Forbes Avenue
Pittsburgh, PA 15282
(412) 396-5000
African-American undergraduate
student body: five percent

**Lafayette College**
118 Markle Hall
Easton, PA 18042
(610) 250-5100
African-American undergraduate
student body: three percent

**La Salle University**
Olney Avenue at 20th Street
Philadelphia, PA 19141
(215) 951-1500
African-American undergraduate
student body: 13 percent

**Lehigh University**
27 Memorial Drive W.
Bethlehem, PA 18015
(610) 758-3100
African-American undergraduate
student body: three percent

**Lincoln University**
Lincoln University, PA 19352
(610) 932-8300
African-American undergraduate
student body: 94 percent

**Penn State University**
University Park Campus
University Park, PA 16802
(814) 865-5471
African-American undergraduate
student body: three percent

**Robert Morris College**
881 Narrows Run Road
Moon Township, PA 15108
(412) 262-8206
African-American undergraduate
student body: seven percent

**St. Joesph's University**
5600 City Avenue
Phildelphia, PA 19131
(610) 660-1300
African-American undergraduate
student body: nine percent

**Temple University**
1801 N. Broad Street
Philadelphia, PA 19122
(215) 204-7200
African-American undergraduate
student body: 28 percent

**University of Pennsylvania**
34th and Spruce Streets
Philadelphia, PA 19104
(215) 898-7507
African-American undergraduate
student body: six percent

**University of Pittsburgh**
4200 Fifth Avenue
Pittsburgh, PA 15260
(412) 624-7488
African-American undergraduate
student body: 10 percent

**Villanova University**
800 Lancaster Avenue
Villanova, PA 19085
(800) 338-7927
African-American undergraduate
student body: two percent

# Rhode Island

**Brown University**
Box 1860
Providence, RI 02912
(401) 863-2378
African-American undergraduate
student body: six percent

**Providence College**
Easton and River Avenues
Providence, RI 02918
(401) 865-2535
African-American undergraduate
student body: two percent

**University of Rhode Island**
121 Carlotti
Kingston, RI 02881
(401) 874-7100
African-American undergraduate
student body: three percent

## Souŧh Carolina

**Benedict College**
Columbia, SC 29204
(803) 256-4220
African-American undergraduate
student body: 97 percent

**Charleston Southern University**
PO Box 118087
8000 University Boulevard
Charleston, SC 29423
(803) 863-7050
African-American undergraduate
student body: 21 percent

**Clemson University**
105 Sikes Hall
Clemson, SC 29634
(864) 656-2287
African-American undergraduate
student body: eight percent

**Coastal Carolina University**
PO Box 261954
Conway, SC 29528
(803) 349-2026
African-American undergraduate
student body: nine percent

**College of Charleston**
66 George Street
Charleston, SC 29424
(803) 953-5670
African-American undergraduate
student body: eight percent

**Furman University**
3300 Poinsett Highway
Greenville, SC 29613
(864) 294-2034
African-American undergraduate
student body: four percent

**Morris College**
Sumter, SC 29150-3599
(803) 775-9371
African-American undergraduate
student body: 100 percent

**South Carolina State University**
300 College Street N.E.
Orangeburg, SC 29117
(803) 536-7185
African-American undergraduate
student body: 96 percent

**The Citadel**
171 Moultrie Street
Charleston, SC 29409
(803) 953-5230
African-American undergraduate
student body: eight percent

**University of South Carolina**
Columbia, SC 29208
(803) 777-7700
African-American undergraduate
student body: 19 percent

**Voorhees College**
Denmark, SC 29042
(803) 793-3351
African-American undergraduate
student body: 98 percent

**Winthrop University**
701 Oakland Avenue
Rock Hill, SC 29733
(803) 323-2191
African-American undergraduate
student body: 22 percent

**Wofford College**
429 N. Church Street
Spartanburg, SC 29303
(864) 597-4130
African-American undergraduate
student body: six percent

## Tennessee

**Austin Peay State University**
601 College Street
Clarksville, TN 37044
(615) 648-7661
African-American undergraduate
student body: 18 percent

**East Tennessee State**
University Parkway
Johnson City, TN 37614
(423) 929-4213
African-American undergraduate
student body: four percent

**Fisk University**
1000-17th Avenue N.
Nashville, TN 37208
(800) 443-3475
African-American undergraduate
student body: 100 percent

**Knoxville College**
Knoxville, TN 37921
(615) 524-6500
African-American undergraduate
student body: 99 percent

**Lane College**
545 Lane Avenue
Jackson, TN 38301
(901) 426-7533
African-American undergraduate
student body: 99 percent

**Le Moyne-Owen College**
807 Walker Avenue
Memphis, TN 38126
(901) 942-7302
African-American undergraduate
student body: 84 percent

**Middle Tennessee State University**
1301 E. Main Street
CAB Room 208
Murfreesboro, TN 37132
(615) 898-2111
African-American undergraduate
student body: 10 percent

**Tennessee State University**
3500 John Merritt Boulevard
Nashville, TN 37209
(615) 963-5105
African-American undergraduate
student body: 76 percent

**University of Memphis**
229 Administration Building
Memphis, TN 38152
(901) 678-2101
African-American undergraduate
student body: 27 percent

**University of Tennessee-Chattanooga**
615 McCallie Avenue
Chattanooga, TN 37403
(423) 755-4662
African-American undergraduate
student body: 14 percent

**University of Tennessee**
320 Student Service Building
Circle Park Drive
Knoxville, TN 37996
(423) 974-2184
African-American undergraduate
student body: five percent

**University of Tennessee-Martin**
Administration Building
Room 201
Martin, TN 38238
(901) 587-7020
African-American undergraduate
student body: 14 percent

**Vanderbilt University**
2305 W. End Avenue
Nashville, TN 37203
(615) 322-2561
African-American undergraduate
student body: four percent

# Texas

**Baylor University**
Waco, TX 76798
(800) 229-5678
African-American undergraduate
student body: five percent

**Huston-Tillotson College**
Austin, TX 78702
(512) 505-3000
African-American undergraduate
student body: 77 percent

**Jarvis Christian College**
Hawkins, TX 75765
(903) 769-5700
African-American undergraduate
student body: 99 percent

**Lamar University**
Lamar Station
Box 10001
Beaumont, TX 77710
(409) 880-8888
African-American undergraduate
student body: 18 percent

**Paul Quinn College**
3837 Simpson Stuart Road
Dallas, TX 75241
(214) 376-1000
African-American undergraduate
student body: N/A

**Prairie View A&M University**
PO Box 3089
Office of Admissions and Records
Prairie View, TX 77446
(409) 857-2618
African-American undergraduate
student body: 90 percent

**Rice University**
6100 Main Street
Houston, TX 77005
(713) 527-4036
African-American undergraduate
student body: seven percent

**Sam Houston State University**
PO Box 2418
Huntsville, TX 77341
(409) 294-1056
African-American undergraduate
student body: 12 percent

**Southern Methodist University**
PO Box 750296
Dallas, TX 75275
(800) 323-0672
African-American undergraduate
student body: six percent

**Southwest Texas State University**
601 University Drive
San Marcos, TX 78666
(512) 245-2364
African-American undergraduate
student body: five percent

**Southwestern Christian College**
Terrell, TX 75160
(214) 524-3341
African-American undergraduate
student body: N/A

**Stephen F. Austin State
University**
SFA Station 13051
Nacogdoches, TX 75962
(409) 468-2504
African-American undergraduate
student body: eight percent

**Texas A&M University**
College Station, TX 77843
(409) 845-3741
African-American undergraduate
student body: three percent

**Texas College**
Tyler, TX 75702
(903) 593-8311
African-American undergraduate
student body: 99 percent

**Texas Southern University**
3100 Cleburne
Houston, TX 77004
(713) 313-1001
African-American undergraduate
student body: 83 percent

**Texas Tech University**
Box 42013
Lubbock, TX 79409
(806) 742-1493
African-American undergraduate
student body: three percent

**University of Houston**
Campus Communications
Houston, TX 77204
(713) 743-1010
African-American undergraduate
student body: 12 percent

**University of North Texas**
PO Box 13797
Denton, TX 76203
(817) 565-2681
African-American undergraduate
student body: eight percent

**University of Texas-Arlington**
701 S. Nedderman Drive
PO Box 19088
Arlington, TX 76019
(817) 272-2225
African-American undergraduate
student body: 10 percent

**University of Texas**
Main Building
Room 7
Austin, TX 78712
(512) 475-7399
African-American undergraduate
student body: four percent

**University of Texas-El Paso**
500 W. University Avenue
El Paso, TX 79968
(915) 747-5576
African-American undergraduate
student body: three percent

**University of Texas-Pan
American**
1201 W. University Drive
Edinburg, TX 78539
(210) 381-2206
African-American undergraduate
student body: N/A

**University of Texas-San Antonio**
6900 N. Loop 1604, W
San Antonio, TX 78249
(800) 669-0919
African-American undergraduate
student body: four percent

**Wiley College**
Marshall, TX 75670
(903) 927-3300
African-American undergraduate
student body: 99 percent

# Utah

**Brigham Young University**
ASB A-153
Provo, UT 84602
(801) 378-2507
African-American undergraduate
student body: zero percent

**Southern Utah University**
351 W. Center
Cedar City, UT 84720
(801) 586-7740
African-American undergraduate
student body: one percent

**University of Utah**
200 S. University Street
Salt Lake City, UT 84112
(801) 581-7281
African-American undergraduate
student body: one percent

**Utah State University**
University Hill
Logan, UT 84322
(801) 797-1079
African-American undergraduate
student body: one percent

**Weber State University**
3750 Harrison Boulevard
Ogden, UT 84408
(801) 626-6743
African-American undergraduate
student body: one percent

# Vermont

**University of Vermont**
South Prospect Street
Burlington, VT 05405
(802) 656-3370
African-American undergraduate
student body: one percent

# Virginia

**College of William and Mary**
PO Box 8795
Williamsburg, VA 23187
(757) 221-4223
African-American undergraduate
student body: six percent

**George Mason University**
4400 University Drive
Fairfax, VA 22030
(703) 993-2395
African-American undergraduate
student body: eight percent

**Hampton University**
Tyler Street
Hampton, VA 23668
(804) 727-5328
African-American undergraduate
student body: N/A

**James Madison University**
Harrisonburg, VA 22807
(540) 568-6147
African-American undergraduate
student body: five percent

**Liberty University**
Box 20000
Lynchburg, VA 24506
(804) 582-2100
African-American undergraduate
student body: N/A

**Norfolk State University**
2401 Corprew Avenue
Norfolk, VA 23504
(757) 683-8396
African-American undergraduate
student body: 88 percent

**Old Dominion University**
5215 Hampton Boulevard
Norfolk, VA 23529
(757) 683-3637
African-American undergraduate
student body: 19 percent

**Radford University**
PO Box 6903
Radford, VA 24142
(540) 831-5371
African-American undergraduate
student body: four percent

**University of Richmond**
28 Westhampton Way
Richmond, VA 23173
(804) 289-8640
African-American undergraduate
student body: six percent

**Saint Paul's College**
Lawrenceville, VA 23868
(804) 848-3111
African-American undergraduate
student body: 93 percent

**University of Virginia**
Office of Admissions
PO Box 9017
Charlottesville, VA 22906
(804) 982-3200
African-American undergraduate
student body: 11 percent

**Virginia Commonwalth
University**
821 W. Franklin Street
Richmond, VA 23285
(800) 841-3638
African-American undergraduate
student body: 21 percent

**Virginia Military Institute**
Lexington, VA 24450
(800) 767-4207
African-American undergraduate
student body: six percent

**Virginia State University**
1 Hayden Place
PO Box 9013
Petersburg, VA 23806
(804) 524-5902
African-American undergraduate
student body: 94 percent

**Virginia Tech**
Office of Admissions
7210 Burruss Hall
Blacksburg, VA 24061
(540) 231-6267
African-American undergraduate
student body: four percent

**Virginia Union University**
1500 N. Lombardy Street
Richmond, VA 23220
(804) 257-5856
African-American undergraduate
student body: 99 percent

# Washington

**Eastern Washington University**
MS 148
Cheney, WA 99004
(509) 359-2397
African-American undergraduate
student body: two percent

**Gonzaga University**
509 E. Boone Avenue
Spokane, WA 99258
(509) 324-5784
African-American undergraduate
student body: one percent

**University of Washington**
Seattle, WA 98195
(206) 543-9686
African-American undergraduate
student body: three percent

**Washington State University**
French Administration Building
Pullman, WA 99164
(509) 335-4902
African-American undergraduate
student body: two percent

# West Virginia

**Bluefield State College**
Bluefield, WV 24701
(304) 327-4000
African-American undergraduate
student body: nine percent

**Marshall University**
400 Hal Greer Boulevard
Huntington, WV 25755
(800) 642-3499
African-American undergraduate
student body: four percent

**West Virginia State College**
Institute, WV 25112-1000
(304) 766-3000
African-American undergraduate
student body: 13 percent

**West Virginia University**
PO Box 6201
President's Office
Morgantown, WV 26506
(800) 344-9881
African-American undergraduate
student body: four percent

# Wisconsin

**Marquette University**
PO Box 1881
Milwaukee, WI 53201
(800) 222-6544
African-American undergraduate
student body: five percent

**University of Wisconsin-Green Bay**
2420 Nicolet Drive
Green Bay, WI 54311
(414) 465-2111
African-American undergraduate
student body: one percent

**University of Wisconsin**
170 Bascom Hall
500 Lincoln Drive
Madison, WI 53706
(608) 262-3961
African-American undergraduate
student body: two percent

**University of Wisconsin-Milwaukee**
PO Box 413
Milwaukee, WI 53201
(414) 229-3800
African-American undergraduate
student body: nine percent

# Wyoming

**University of Wyoming**
PO Box 3314
Old Main 321
Laramie, WY 82071
(307) 766-5160
African-American undergraduate
student body: one percent

## The Top 25 men's basketball programs

1. Duke
2. North Carolina
3. Kansas
4. UCLA
5. Kentucky
6. Michigan
7. Arizona
8. Syracuse
9. Indiana
10. Louisville
11. Georgetown
12. Cincinnati
13. Villanova
14. Arkansas
15. Connecticut
16. Iowa
17. Georgia Tech
18. Temple
19. Illinois
20. Utah
21. Iowa State
22. Texas
23. Clemson
24. UNLV
25. New Mexico

## The Top 25 women's basketball programs

1. Tennessee
2. Louisiana Tech
3. Stanford
4. Iowa
5. Alabama
6. Georgia
7. Notre Dame
8. Florida
9. Colorado
10. Connecticut
11. Old Dominion
12. Penn State
13. Vanderbilt
14. Virginia
15. Texas
16. Western Kentucky
17. Duke
18. Kansas
19. Wisconsin
20. Washington
21. Mississippi
22. Memphis
23. Southern Miss
24. Purdue
25. Texas Tech

## The Top 25 football programs

1. Florida
2. Penn State
3. Nebraska
4. Notre Dame
5. Tennessee
6. Ohio State
7. Florida State
8. Washington
9. Texas
10. North Carolina
11. LSU
12. Syracuse
13. Miami
14. Michigan
15. Alabama
16. Auburn
17. USC
18. Clemson
19. Michigan State
20. Stanford
21. Virginia Tech
22. Colorado
23. Northwestern
24. BYU
25. Iowa

Notes:

# ORDER FORM

**Fax Orders:**           602-283-0991
**Telephone Orders:**     602-460-1660
**Online Orders: E-mail:** Amberbk@aol.com
**Postal Orders:** Send Checks and Money Orders to:
      **Amber Books Publishing**
      **1334 East Chandler Blvd., Suite 5-D67**
      **Phoenix, AZ 85048**

Please send _____ copy/ies of "How to Play the Sports Recruiting Game and Get an Athletic Scholarship: The Handbook and Guide to Success for the African-American High School Student-Athlete" by Rodney J. McKissic.

Please send _____ copy/ies of "Is Modeling for You? The Handbook and Guide for the Young Aspiring Black Model" by Yvonne Rose and Tony Rose.

Name: _____
Company Name: _____
Address: _____
City: _____ State: _____ Zip: _____
Telephone: (_____) _____

Sports Recruiting:   $12.95
Modeling:            $14.95

❑ Check    ❑ Money Order    ❑ Cashiers Check
Payable to Amber Books, 1334 E. Chandler Blvd., Suite 5-D67, Phoenix, AZ 85048

**Shipping:**   $5.00 per book. Allow 7 days for delivery.
**Sales Tax:** Add 7.05% to books shipped to Arizona addresses.
**Total enclosed:** $_____

**For Bulk Rates Call:** 602-460-1660

# ORDER NOW

# ORDER FORM

**Fax Orders:**  602-283-0991
**Telephone Orders:**  602-460-1660
**Online Orders: E-mail:**  Amberbk@aol.com
**Postal Orders:** Send Checks and Money Orders to:
**Amber Books Publishing**
**1334 East Chandler Blvd., Suite 5-D67**
**Phoenix, AZ 85048**

Please send _____ copy/ies of "How to Play the Sports Recruiting Game and Get an Athletic Scholarship: The Handbook and Guide to Success for the African-American High School Student-Athlete" by Rodney J. McKissic.

Please send _____ copy/ies of "Is Modeling for You? The Handbook and Guide for the Young Aspiring Black Model" by Yvonne Rose and Tony Rose.

Name: _____

Company Name: _____

Address: _____

City: _____ State: _____ Zip: _____

Telephone: ( ___ ) _____

Sports Recruiting:  $12.95
Modeling:  $14.95

❏ Check  ❏ Money Order  ❏ Cashiers Check
Payable to Amber Books, 1334 E. Chandler Blvd., Suite 5-D67, Phoenix, AZ 85048

**Shipping:**  $5.00 per book. Allow 7 days for delivery.
**Sales Tax:** Add 7.05% to books shipped to Arizona addresses.
**Total enclosed:**  $_____

**For Bulk Rates Call:** 602-460-1660

# ORDER NOW

# ORDER FORM

**Fax Orders:**            602-283-0991
**Telephone Orders:**      602-460-1660
**Online Orders: E-mail:**  Amberbk@aol.com
**Postal Orders:** Send Checks and Money Orders to:
**Amber Books Publishing**
**1334 East Chandler Blvd., Suite 5-D67**
**Phoenix, AZ 85048**

Please send _____ copy/ies of "How to Play the Sports Recruiting Game and Get an Athletic Scholarship: The Handbook and Guide to Success for the African-American High School Student-Athlete" by Rodney J. McKissic.

Please send _____ copy/ies of "Is Modeling for You? The Handbook and Guide for the Young Aspiring Black Model" by Yvonne Rose and Tony Rose.

Name: _____
Company Name: _____
Address: _____
City: _____ State: _____ Zip: _____
Telephone: (      ) _____

Sports Recruiting:  $12.95
Modeling:           $14.95

❑ Check    ❑ Money Order    ❑ Cashiers Check
Payable to Amber Books, 1334 E. Chandler Blvd., Suite 5-D67, Phoenix, AZ 85048

**Shipping:**   $5.00 per book. Allow 7 days for delivery.
**Sales Tax:** Add 7.05% to books shipped to Arizona addresses.
**Total enclosed:** $_____

**For Bulk Rates Call:** 602-460-1660

# ORDER NOW

Notes:

Rodney J. McKissic is known nationally as a college basketball authority and an award-winning sports writer and journalist. McKissic is a graduate of the University of Cincinnati with a degree in broadcasting. He is currently the national college basketball writer for *The News Tribune* in Tacoma, WA. where he resides with his wife Tracia, son Asher, and daughter Dru.